"My clients constantly ask me, 'What can I snack on with Paleo?' and I usually respond, 'Fruit and nuts.' Thanks to Landria's book however, I can now add Bacon and Egg Maple Muffins, Sweet Potato Power Brownies, and Homemade Beef Jerky to the list!"

—**TONY FEDERICO,** ACSM HFS, CFL1, author of *Paleo Grilling*

"*Super Paleo Snacks* is a beautiful cookbook filled with many wonderful, healthy, and delicious Paleo snack ideas. This book is your solution to finding ideas for Paleo snacking and there is something for just about everyone. Landria has done an amazing job and this is a great addition to your Paleo cookbook collection that I promise you will use time after time."

—**HEATHER CONNELL,** author of *Paleo Sweets and Treats*

"Landria's Paleo cookbook offers many of the classic Paleo favorites plus some cool surprises, using Paleo ingredients that are rich in natural sweeteners, proteins, and healthy fats. You'll never run out of snack ideas with *Super Paleo Snacks*."

—**ERICA KERWIEN,** author of *The Healthy Coconut Flour Cookbook*

Super Paleo Snacks

100 Delicious Low-Glycemic, Gluten-Free Snacks That Will Make Living Your Paleo Lifestyle Simple & Satisfying

LANDRIA VOIGT, C.H.H.C.

FAIR WINDS

Quarto is the authority on a wide range of topics.

Quarto educates, entertains and enriches the lives of our readers—enthusiasts and lovers of hands-on living.

www.QuartoKnows.com

First published in the USA in 2015 by
Fair Winds Press, an imprint of
Quarto Publishing Group USA Inc.
100 Cummings Center
Suite 406-L
Beverly, MA 01915-6101

QuartoKnows.com
Visit our blogs at QuartoKnows.com

18 17 16   3 4 5

ISBN: 978-1-59233-647-0

Digital edition published in 2015
eISBN: 978-1-62788-191-3

Library of Congress Cataloging-in-Publication Data

Voigt, Landria.
  Super paleo snacks : 100 delicious low-glycemic, gluten-free snacks that will make living your paleo lifestyle simple & satisfying / Landria Voigt, C.H.H.C.
    pages cm
  ISBN 978-1-59233-647-0 (paperback)
  1. Low-carbohydrate diet--Recipes. 2. Gluten-free diet--Recipes. 3. Snack foods. 4. Natural foods. 5. Prehistoric people--Nutrition. 6. Quick and easy cooking. I. Title.

  RM237.73.V65 2015
  641.5'6383--dc23
                              2014025752

Cover and book design by
Laura McFadden Design, Inc.
Photography by Landria Voigt

Printed and bound in China

The information in this book is for educational purposes only. It is not intended to replace the advice of a physician or medical practitioner. Please see your health care provider before beginning any new health program.

To my loves, Scott, Alice, and Tate.

CONTENTS

① THE IMPORTANCE OF HEALTHY SNACKING 14

- Why We Snack
- How to Snack
- Let's Start Shopping

② SCHOOL AND WORK SNACKS 34

Nourishing Snacks to Keep You Focused and Full All Day Long

36 Savory Baked Chicken Nuggets

39 Bacon & Egg Maple Muffins

40 Pigs in a Blanket

42 Bacon Cauliflower Soup

43 Homemade Beef Jerky

44 Sun-Dried Tomato Chicken Sliders

47 Cauliflower Pizza Bites

48 Chicken Maple Sausage Meatballs

49 Mediterranean Bread

51 Egg Muffins

52 Mexican Muffins

53 Teriyaki Salmon Cakes

55 Buffalo Chicken Wings

56 Italian Meatballs

59 Apple Crumb Bites

60 Blonde Snack Bars

61 Pumpkin Chocolate Chip Muffins

63 Supersmart Bars

64 Cinnamon Blueberry Bread

65 Blueberry Muffins

③ AT-HOME SNACKS 66

Use Your Home-Field Advantage for the Tastiest and Healthiest Snack Options

68 Crispy Okra Sticks

71 Green Deviled Eggs & Bacon

72 Kale Salad

75 Cauliflower Hummus

76 Easy "Cheesy" Kale Chips

77 Creamy Zucchini

78 Butternut Squash Fritters

81 Prosciutto-Wrapped Asparagus

82 Squash Chips

83 Onion Rings

84 Zesty Walnut Brussels Sprouts

87 Sweet Bacon Kale

88 Soft Paleo Pretzels

90 Ranch "Cheese" Ball

91 Roasted Red Pepper Dip

92 Artichoke Pesto

93 Pancake-Wrapped Sausage

95 Green Lemonade Smoothie

96 Easy-Bake Cake Cup

97 Energizing Chocolate Milk or Hot Chocolate

④ ON-THE-GO SNACKS 98

Fun and Convenient Treats for Road Trips, Commutes, and Carpools

100 Cinnamon Graham Crackers

102 Chocolate Almond Squares

103 Chocolate Chip Granola Squares

105 Pumpkin Bars

106 Almond Cheese Crackers

108 Buttered Saltine Crackers

109 Apple Crisp Chips

111 Silver Dollar Banana Pancakes

112 Crispy Maple Granola

114 My Favorite Crunchy Crackers

115 Flatcake Sandwich Bread

116 Superfruity Roll-Ups

117 Pinwheel Sandwich Bread

119 Raw Coconut Almond Bonbons

120 Strawberry Gummies

122 Cinnamon Bun Biscuits

123 Chocolate Chip Muffins

124 Cinnamon Raisin Bars

125 Mini Zucchini Muffins

5

ENERGY-REPLENISHING SNACKS 126
Pre- and Postworkout Foods That Provide Quick Fuel and Fast Recovery

128 Sweet Potato Power Brownies

130 Banana-Blueberry Power Squares

131 Cherry-Cacao Energy Balls

132 Crunchy Granola Brittle

133 Honey Almond Nut Butter

134 Banana Nut Bites

135 Powerhouse Paleo Coffee

137 Chocolate Chia Workout Bars

138 Crunchy Sweet Potato Fries

141 Chocolate Banana Smoothie

142 Banana Walnut Muffins

143 Sweet Potato Casserole Bread

144 Bacon & Sweet Potato Hash

145 Chocolate Muffins

146 Chia Pudding

147 Sweet Potato Pancakes

6

NUT-FREE SNACKS 148
Scrumptious Paleo Snacks without Tree Nuts or Peanuts

150 Pumpkin-Spiced Granola Bars

152 Apple Pie Trail Mix Balls

153 Crunchy Omega-3 Flax Granola

155 "Peanut Butter" Patties

156 Best Nut-Free Muffins Around

157 Chocolate Sunflower Seed Butter

158 Flatbread "PB&J"

159 Crispy Four-Seed Granola

160 Sweet & Salty Spiced Pepitas

163 "Peanut Butter" Cookies

164 Chocolate Zucchini "Bread"

165 Pizza Pockets

7

SWEET TREATS 166
Heavenly Little Snacks without the Guilt

168 Mint Chocolate Chip Balls

169 Blonde Macaroons

170 Mini Peanut Butter Banana Cups

173 Vanilla Cupcakes with Chocolate Frosting

174 Cinnamon Donut Holes

176 "Cheesecake" Bites with Caramel Sauce

177 Happy Birthday Cookie Cake

179 Minty Thins

180 N'Oatmeal Cookies

182 Molten Lava Cakes

183 Apple Crumble

184 Chocolate-Covered Cookies

185 Snickerdoodle Cookie Dough Bites

FRONT

FOREWORD 8

INTRODUCTION 10
• A Little about Me
• Why Paleo?

BACK

INDEX 186

ACKNOWLEDGMENTS 190

ABOUT THE AUTHOR 191

FOREWORD

I can track my knowledge of nutrition by the snacks I pack for my children, now ages five and six. My early understanding (or perhaps misunderstanding) of what constituted "healthy" resulted in snacks that were labeled organic, or in our case, gluten-free. In those days, I didn't know to check for sugar content, protein, and healthy fats.

Today, a little older and definitely wiser, I have become more conscious of what my children and I consume for snacks. Most of the "snacks" that are marketed to our kids not only have little to no nutrition but also contain ingredients that can damage our guts and intestinal lining and, in turn, negatively impact developing brains and bodies. It is crucial that we give our children the proper nutrients (and cut out anti-nutrient foods) so they can reach their full potential.

Healthy snacking isn't just for kids. As adults, our bodies still need optimal nutrition to work and parent effectively. I have a busy schedule that includes seeing patients all day long, writing for various health publications, and media appearances. I need to feel the best I can and stay tack sharp. Because food has such an immediate effect on how I feel, what I snack on is very important. It can make or break my day. I also don't have much time to stop throughout the day so whenever I do get a chance to eat something, I need it to be nutritionally dense and fill me for the long haul as I never know when I will have time to eat again.

Landria's snacks are great because they are full of important healthy fats that help provide fuel throughout the day. Not to mention these recipes are easy-to-make and taste amazing. I love that I, and my kids, can have a sweet potato brownie for a snack and we get a low-glycemic treat that is full of fiber, protein, and other healthy ingredients—not processed sugar, artificial ingredients, or empty calories.

I see patients from all over the world, who, before coming to see me, have sought help through traditional medicine. Unfortunately, more often than not, these patients have been prescribed strong prescription drugs, replete with side effects, to alleviate symptoms. I believe we should find the root cause of the problem—not prescribe away the symptoms—in order to get a solution. As a first step for all my patients, I start by assessing their diet. I have witnessed firsthand just how important food is to our health and how it can affect our bodies dramatically. I have seen food heal autoimmune diseases, diabetes, chronic pain, and even help with mental issues like ADHD, anxiety, and depression.

Of course, eating well can be a challenge for many. I cannot count the number of times patients have looked at me blankly, wondering what they should eat now that I have told them to be gluten-free or dairy-free or adopt some other diet modification. Knowing what to make and finding time to make it can be tremendous obstacles to healthy eating. I know for myself, as well as for my two young children, that coming up with healthy snacks on a daily basis can be especially daunting.

Knowing Landria as both a patient and a nutritional consultant at my practice, I can attest to her deep knowledge of nutrition and personal understanding of just how much and what kinds of food can not only heal us, but also enable us to feel and be our best. Landria is knowledgeable and passionate, but probably most importantly, has young children who need healthy snacks. Her recommendations and recipes are nutritionally sound but also practical. She understands that the key to a healthy diet is consistency and sustainability. Recipes that are difficult to make, or too expensive, too time-consuming, or that don't pass the taste test, won't be part of your diet—and the gap will probably be filled by non-nutritious alternatives.

With Landria's supertasty but also very thoughtful recipes, easy-to-follow directions, and beautiful mouthwatering pictures, she makes eating well so much easier, and honestly, even fun! I hope that you will benefit from her unique approach to food and nutrition, just as our patients continue to learn from her daily.

DR. TASNEEM BHATIA, M.D.
author of *What Doctors Eat* and *The Belly Fix*

INTRODUCTION

When most Americans reach for a snack, odds are pretty good that it's going to be an unhealthy one, laden with processed sugars, gluten, hydrogenated oil, and unpronounceable chemicals. I believe it's the allure of convenience, and not willful ignorance, that is the true driver behind this trend. After all, we are an on-the-go society, and grabbing that bag of chips or a handful of cheese-flavored crackers is so much easier than taking a few minutes to prepare something healthy.

But there's a better way.

Snacks are an *essential* part of our daily diet, and *Super Paleo Snacks* will provide you with an array of healthy options—including grab-and-go staples and out-of-the-box alternatives to junk food. All of the snacks in these pages are made with real food, nourishing oils, and the kinds of ingredients that help blood sugars stay balanced. They're quick and easy to make—most take less than 10 minutes to prepare. And, most important, they are delicious!

A Little about Me

I am a wife and mother of two, a nutritional consultant and public speaker, a professional photographer, and the author of a kid-friendly Paleo blog, stiritup.me.

Though I have had a passion for nutrition for as long as I can remember, I came to realize the importance and true power of food firsthand. For years, I battled debilitating bouts of ulcerative colitis and other autoimmune diseases. It seemed like doctors prescribed every drug and steroid under the sun, and instead of healing me or taming my symptoms, they actually made me sicker.

In a fit of desperation, I changed my eating habits, embraced a "real foods" (or as some call it, a Paleo) diet, and within days, my years of health issues *finally* came to an end. To me, it was nothing short of a miracle. Those six prescription pills my doctor ordered me to take every day for the rest of my life, the ones that actually made me sicker with other issues, haven't touched my tongue since I changed my diet.

I have spent the years since then studying how food dramatically affects our mental and physical health. I've always said, "It's hard to ignore what you know." And so, armed with an understanding of food's importance on our well-being, it was impossible for me not to change my family's nutritional lifestyle for the better.

I must confess, though, if someone had told me five years ago that I would be authoring a cookbook, I would have fallen over laughing. Not only was I incompetent in the kitchen, but also I found cooking to be an absolutely disagreeable endeavor. But for the sake of my and my family's health, I began to prepare all of our meals.

Much to my surprise, over the years, I have actually come to love cooking. For me, there is profound delight in trying to find the most efficient way to concoct a tasty meal. But just because I like cooking it doesn't mean that I want to spend a lot of time doing it. And so, through trial and error, I've learned to be more efficient.

But even more fulfilling is the thrill that comes when an experimental recipe works. There is almost nothing more satisfying to me than hearing, "This is yummy, Mommy," mumbled through a mouthful of an experiment gone right. That, and knowing that I am doing what I can to nourish my family as best I can, is both satisfying and motivating to keep me at it.

Why Paleo?

After years of ineffective medications and treatments, I feel the Paleo diet saved me from a life of pain and disease. If you're new to the Paleolithic diet ("Paleo" for short), a brief overview is probably in order.

The Paleo diet, also referred to as the "Caveman diet," derives both its name and its core dietary guidelines from the premise that our bodies are optimized to process simple, natural whole foods—foods that, theoretically, a caveman living in the Paleolithic era would have hunted or gathered.

Most Paleo followers chafe at the caveman rule, as it vastly oversimplifies what is, in truth, a much more scientifically designed approach to nutrition. The Paleo diet carefully considers not just the nutrients that our bodies need but also the manner in which our bodies process and digest proteins, fats, and carbohydrates. Following a whole-foods diet rich in healthy fats actually encourages sustainable weight loss and has been shown to be helpful in managing diabetes, preventing heart disease, and even improving focus in individuals with ADHD.

If you really think about it, the Paleo diet is as much about what you are not eating as it is what you are. The industrialization of food production that has taken place over the past 150 years has introduced into our diet an onslaught of chemicals and derivations of traditional ingredients (refined white sugar, for example) that our body struggles to digest. These new "foods" have a tight correlation with the rise in food allergies and autoimmune diseases such as rheumatoid arthritis. Further, science is just starting to fully appreciate and understand how these foods inflame the gut and trigger a whole range of health issues. No wonder there are so many miraculous stories, similar to mine, of autoimmune diseases ending as soon as someone makes the leap to Paleo.

More important, the health benefits associated with leaving grains and legumes behind are immense. Grains and grain intolerance are now tied to numerous afflictions, including celiac disease, endometriosis, infertility, heart disease, joint pain, arthritis, mental disorders, skin conditions, headaches, migraines, and more. So, it might be worth asking, "Is pizza really worth it?"

If you did an Internet search for "Paleo diet," you might quickly note that there is a wide-ranging set of opinions about which foods are and are not considered acceptable. It is generally agreed that fish, meats, veg -etables, fruit, nuts, and some tubers are Paleo, while dairy, processed sugar, grains, legumes, and white potatoes are not. Paleo also places an emphasis on organically farmed foods and grass-fed meats.

The recipes in this book generally adhere to these classifications. It is worth noting, however, that there are a few recipes that call for psyllium husk powder and nutritional yeast, which some followers of Paleo might contend are not Paleo compliant. It is my belief that both psyllium husk and nutritional yeast are natural and have positive health benefits (see "Let's Start Shopping," page 19).

As I see it, Paleo doesn't have to be a way of eating with so many strict rules. Rather, it's a great guideline for clean eating. Being strictly Paleo can be difficult, and even the most ardent in the Paleo community recognize the need to occasionally "cheat." Many recommend following the 90/10 or 80/20 rule, meaning to eat Paleo foods 80 to 90 percent of the time. But, because our genes are different and our bodies react very differently to food, it's up to every person to figure out what diet is going to work best.

Consider the Peanut

In a couple of recipes, I note that peanut butter can be substituted for almond butter because kids tend to love it. Peanuts are actually a legume and thus not considered Paleo. But, in my opinion, it is much more important to serve a healthy snack than to dogmatically adhere to a dietary philosophy. As long as your body can tolerate a food and the food can be consumed in moderation, it isn't worth worrying too much about its "Paleoness."

THE IMPORTANCE
OF HEALTHY SNACKING

Everyone snacks. Okay, maybe not everyone, but almost everyone. In fact, a 2010 study in the *Journal of Nutrition* found that 97 percent of Americans do nosh between meals. Moreover, the study concluded that 24 percent—nearly a quarter—of our total energy intake comes from snacks. But for something that contributes to our diet as much as breakfast, lunch, and dinner do, it's somewhat surprising that relatively few people know whether they are following good snacking habits—or even that there is such a thing as a "good snack habit."

Most snacks consumed today skew toward the prepackaged and processed kinds. Consuming empty calories—those that add calories but little else—that are high in refined sugar, white flour, gluten, and food coloring is, in general, bad for you.

If we were to go back 2,000 years, we would note that food's primary function was to sustain one's life. No food; no life. Food was simply calories to be consumed. Of course, this remains true today, though thankfully, the threat of starvation seems to be a distant concern for most people in the industrialized world. Yet, for many of us, our lizard brains still perform the same calculus as our distant ancestors' brains did when presented with something to eat: calories equal life, so dig in.

But in the past fifty years, something significant happened to the composition of our food, and our consumption paradigm shifted. Real foods—natural fats, leafy vegetables, ripe fruit, grass-fed beef—were replaced with industrial foods. These new foods were cheaper to make on a larger scale, and therefore cheaper to buy. Butter took a backseat to margarine. Fast-food chains began dotting the landscape. Pesticides found their way onto our plates. Hormones and antibiotics began to impact not just the animal, but also the eater of the animal. Food scientists and marketers capitalized on the opportunity to hack our palates with foods both sweet

Beyond the Gluten-Free Label

Highly refined, gluten-containing flours and grains have an anti-nutrient effect on the body, raise insulin levels, and are inflammatory to the gut, which in turn is bad for the whole body. Unfortunately, deciphering whether something has gluten in it is not an easy task. In addition to the label "gluten-free," you must carefully search for words like wheat, barley, rye, durham, bulgur, malt extract, and many others. It can be tough to decode and easy to miss because gluten is everywhere, including in ketchup, deli meats, salad dressing, and even skin care products. That leaves us with really only one good option when it comes to healthy snacks: making them.

and salty to make them perfectly addictive. For the industrial food complex, profit mattered more than nutrition.

We are just now waking up to a new world in which the elegant simplicity of the food-equals-life equation has become much more nuanced. In this new environment, all foods are not created equal. There are those that sustain and those that inflame. So when it comes to choosing snacks, it is worth asking, What are we about to put into our bodies?

WHY WE SNACK

It is important to understand that snacking is not only normal, but it is also an absolutely healthy endeavor, *as long as the nutritional value of the snack is beneficial.* We snack for many reasons, the primary of which is to stave off hunger in between meals. But there are also physical and cognitive perks that snacking provides.

Snacking can boost cognitive focus throughout the work and school day by helping us maintain blood sugar levels. Our bodies digest whole foods that include fats, proteins, and fiber at a slower and more consistent rate, and therefore release a steadier stream of glucose to the brain. Conversely, a snack that is high in refined sugar and white flour will spike insulin levels and cause one to be more hungry and less focused in a shorter time. The snacks in this book, particularly those in chapter 2, contain ingredients, such as meat, eggs, and nuts, that will hold hunger at bay while keeping you tack sharp.

Another benefit of snacking is that it helps prevent overeating at mealtime. There's a difference between "ruining your dinner" and preparing your body with vital nutrients. Sitting down to dinner with that "I'm famished" feeling can lead you to consume more calories than you actually need. In a state of heightened hunger, you tend to eat faster. Numerous studies have shown that individuals who eat slower typically consume fewer calories than their fast-eating peers. Science suggests this is because of a communication lag between the receptors in your stomach and those in your brain—in other words, between having a full stomach and the *realization* that you're satiated. So by helping quell the feeling of hunger through more consistent engagement of stomach receptors, appropriate pre-meal snacks might actually help you lose weight.

For anyone who works out or plays a sport, preworkout snacks are imperative to optimizing performance. The right balance of protein can help us keep our mind focused and increase endurance by slowing muscle breakdown during activity. Also important is having the right postworkout snacks in your bag. We lose many minerals through the excretion of sweat during exercise, and those minerals need to be replaced quickly so our bodies can work efficiently. With a deficiency of certain minerals, such as magnesium, we may have fatigue, muscle cramps, trouble maintaining blood sugar levels, and a harder time getting oxygen into our muscle cells. Further, Paleo-safe starches and carbohydrates, such as sweet potatoes, can restore glycogen levels in our muscles and get them ready for the next workout. I've dedicated chapter 5 to snacks that are specifically formulated to deliver quick-release energy and reduce the time for muscle recovery.

But, of course, there are also numerous emotional reasons that we nibble throughout the day: when it's time to take a break, when we're bored, when celebrating with others, or, perhaps, when we're just feeling a little blue. To me, letting snacks play an occasional role beyond nutrition is a perfectly normal pattern of behavior. Of course, it is imperative that we remain mindful of the frequency and nutritional composition of emotional eats, and make smart choices. By choosing whole-food healthy snacks, like the ones in this book, you can feel good eating them, knowing you won't crash later in the day.

HOW TO SNACK

One of the main reasons that there isn't a universal guidebook to snacking is that snacking patterns vary greatly based on the needs of an individual. The snacking frequency of a rambunctious two-year-old who is growing like a weed should be vastly different from a sedate fifty-something office worker. Moreover, the snacking goals of individuals with blood sugar issues differ from those of someone trying to manage weight. That said, there are a few guidelines that anyone can follow.

You might not expect this bit of advice from a book about snacks, but—at least when it comes to adults—I generally recommend that you skip the snack if you don't need it. But how do you know if you need it? What signals should you look for?

For starters, if you feel even slightly hungry, go ahead and have a snack. Unless, of course, your next meal is within an hour or you are munching on some healthy real-food veggies. In my mind, vegetables are never off-limits.

When you really think about it, though, what is it to "feel hungry"? The signs are usually much more subtle than a rumbling tummy, which can often be quelled by a glass of water, as many times we mistake thirst for hunger. Is your energy starting to wane? Perhaps your ability to focus on the task at hand is becoming more of a challenge. Are you becoming a bit more irritable? When any of these symptoms start to surface, it's snack time.

Knowing how big or small a snack should be is somewhat subjective, especially if you are adhering to the Paleo diet. Many Paleo gurus will tell you to ignore counting calories because when you eat natural foods, your body is much better at sending "full" signals to your brain, thereby preventing overeating. So listen to your body. It's a snack, not a meal. You should come away from a snack feeling satisfied, not stuffed. Yet, for some of us, it is hard to recognize when to say when, so a general rule of thumb would be to consume no more than 200 or so calories per snack.

I'm often asked by my clients who struggle to interpret the hunger signals from their bodies for a snack plan that provides a bit more structure to their daily routine. My advice: for an average person of average size, a basic snacking plan would entail two snacks a day, the first about halfway between breakfast and lunch and the second about halfway between lunch and dinner. It's really as simple as that.

I also generally counsel my clients to close the kitchen at 7 p.m. In the evening after dinner, as you subconsciously prepare for slumber, your body enters a fasting process during which your metabolic rate and digestive process slow significantly, sort of like a bear preparing to hibernate through the winter. If you're watching television or paying bills with a bag of chips on hand, then you're facing two strikes: first with the empty calories and second when your body doesn't burn them as fast.

This includes the "midnight snack." If you're waking up hungry, then you really are not getting enough to eat during the day. Are you eating a good breakfast? Are you snacking at all? I'd suggest adding a little more fiber to your afternoon snack or dinner. This will digest more slowly and should keep you filled overnight. Of course, it is fine to wake up with an appetite for breaking your fast with breakfast.

Little Snacks for Little Ones

Snacks for kids are a completely different story. Young children don't yet know how to interpret or communicate their hunger signals. As such, it is important for you to have a structured snack plan in place. Having a set snack time prevents kids from grazing all day. Grazing, in my opinion, is not a healthy snacking practice. Over the years, consistent grazing begins to abstract the child's awareness of the relationship between food and hunger. Research by the American Academy of Pediatrics suggests that as grazing children mature, they struggle to appropriately self-regulate with food and are more likely to become overeaters.

Now is the perfect time to set kids on the right path of healthy snacking. For kids, two snacks a day are necessary to aid in growth and supply energy. Also, children perform better when they maintain consistent sleeping and eating routines. Therefore, try to maintain a consistent snack time that is evenly interspersed between breakfast and lunch and lunch and dinner.

Their snacks should consist of between 100 and 200 calories, depending on their age and activity level. Try to include protein and healthy fats for them as well, but also be sure to offer them good sources of veggies to ensure they are getting adequate servings per day. Whether it's as simple as providing apple wedges or celery sticks with nut butter or preparing any of the recipes in this book, if you plan for kids to eat something other than processed animal-shaped cookies, crackers, or fruity chews, they'll feel great and be able to perform at their best.

LET'S START SHOPPING

A big goal of this book is to make sure that snack preparation is easy and convenient for you. If you decided to flip open *Super Paleo Snacks* on a cold and rainy day to cook up a quick bite for some hungry kids, only to find that you don't have the right ingredients on hand, dashing to the store would be anything but easy or convenient. In this section, I'll walk you through the staple ingredients, supplies, and gadgets that any Paleo chef should have on hand in the kitchen. I'll also suggest some substitute ingredients, just in case. Most of these ingredients can be found in a natural foods store, the natural foods section of many grocery stores, or online.

Baking Flours

If you are new to Paleo, you might think all flours are created equal. They aren't. Traditional wheat flour can be remarkably detrimental to your health. It contains a specific starch, amylopectin, that is closely linked to weight gain and obesity. Further, wheat starch is laden with gluten, which causes inflammation even in individuals who don't have a specifically diagnosed gluten allergy. Fortunately, there is a range of healthy, whole-food alternatives to wheat flour that are low-glycemic, low-carb, and high in protein.

Almond flour: Almond flour is great for baking because it can yield a very bread-like texture in muffins or a crusty consistency in crackers. Of course, almonds are rich in antioxidants, low in carbohydrates, and high in healthy monounsaturated fats, which are good for the heart. If possible, use blanched almond flour, which uses skinless almonds. Blanched is preferable because almond skins hold some antinutrients (see "How to Use Nuts," page 22). The blanched also tend to look better in baked goods. If using almond flour as a substitute for wheat flour, you can use a 1:1 ratio in most recipes.

Almond meal: Almond meal is prepared by simply grinding whole almonds into a coarser texture than almond flour. Because the texture is coarser, it serves as a great replacement for bread crumbs. I like to use it on my chicken nuggets, meat loaves, or even with some heavier baked goods such as oatmeal cookies.

Coconut flour: High in fiber, low in carbohydrates, and full of protein, this flour is great to use because it can help make Paleo treats light and fluffy. Just know that if you are using it as a substitute ingredient, coconut flour is quite absorptive. You may need additional eggs or liquid to avoid having recipes come out dry. This is actually helpful if we are trying to get extra protein in a snack. The rule of thumb when using coconut flour is to add 1 egg (or 1 tablespoon fat) per 1 tablespoon coconut flour.

Arrowroot powder: Arrowroot is made from the dehydrated arrowroot tuber. It is a great natural thickener, generally used to thicken sauces, and can replace cornstarch at a 1:1 ratio. But if using it to replace white or wheat flour, you will want to use a 1:2 ratio (1 tablespoon of arrowroot powder for every 2 tablespoons of all-purpose flour). While this is the only flour that I use that has a higher glycemic load, I use it sparingly. It also can help make baked goods light and fluffy on the inside and crispy on the outside.

Nut and Seed Butters

Nut butters are a fantastic baking ingredient because they can yield a rich, dense baked good. Some of my favorite cookies, muffins, and brownies are made with nut butters. The texture resembles that of a traditional treat. They also serve well as a binder in raw treats.

Almond butter: This nut butter is a great ingredient for baked goods, giving them a smooth texture. It also makes for a great binder for some raw Paleo snacks. Like almond flour, almond butter is high in monounsaturated fat, as well as protein. I prefer to use almond butter rather than dates (the typical Paleo binder for raw snacks) because dates, while natural, are still high in glycemic loads and can spike blood sugar levels.

Sunflower seed butter: This nut-free substitute is made from sunflower seeds and is full of vitamin E, zinc, iron, protein, and fiber. It is great for any recipe that calls for almond (or peanut) butter. Note that when you combine sunflower seed butter with baking soda and then bake it, a chemical reaction will likely turn your snack dark green. It's completely safe to eat; it just looks a little odd. To lessen the greenness, add some lemon juice or reduce the amount of baking soda.

Coconut butter: Blended coconut meat makes for a smooth and creamy coconut butter, which is great for eating alone or as a thickener or binder. Coconut also has natural antibacterial and antiviral properties that can lend a boost to your immune system.

Cashew butter: Like almond butter, cashew butter is fantastic when used in baked goods. It adds a wonderful flavor and helps create a fluffy texture. You can also use raw cashews to make homemade cashew butter, cashew milk, or cashew flour by simply grinding them up in a blender or food processor. Cashews are high in copper, which keeps the blood vessels, nerves, immune system, and bones healthy. It also has selenium, which is good for thyroid function, and zinc, which helps fight infections.

Super Seeds

Raw or toasted, seeds are an excellent way to add brain-building oils like DHA and omega-3s to your diet. They are a solid substitute for nuts if you need to prepare something nut-free, and they add a satisfying crunch to almost any snack.

Flaxseed and flaxseed meal: Flaxseeds are either golden or brown. While their nutritional value and usage are very similar, the golden does tend to have a bit of a milder flavor. Flaxseeds are loaded with omega-3s and

How to Use Nuts

Nuts, especially raw nuts, contain nutritional inhibitors (sometimes called antinutrients) that can put a strain on the digestive system. By soaking the nuts in salt water for at least 7 hours, antinutrients begin to break down, the nuts become easier to digest, and their nutrients are more easily absorbed. I recommend soaking and roasting all nuts for the recipes in advance, if time permits. Fortunately, it is very easy to do. In a large bowl, add enough warm or hot filtered water to submerge all the nuts and mix in 1 tablespoon (18 g) sea salt to every 4 cups (580 g) nuts. Allow to soak for 7 to 18 hours. Then rinse them in a strainer with some cool water. Dry the nuts by either using a dehydrator or putting them in a 150°F (65°C) oven. Most nuts will need between 12 and 24 hours of drying time. Be sure to get them completely dry to avoid mold. I find that the drying process makes the nuts extra crunchy and flavorful.

When cooking or roasting them in a recipe, use raw nuts so you can control how much they are cooked to protect them from overcooking. This will also really bring out their full flavor. If using them in a raw recipe, use roasted nuts to reduce some of the phytic acid, the nutritional inhibitor, and help ease digestion.

fiber, and because of its high density of nutrients, it is often referred to as a "superfood." Many believe that it can reduce the risk of breast cancer in women and prostate cancer in men. While it is a great nut replacement in some nut-free snacks, it can also serve as a substitute for eggs as a binder. Use about 3 tablespoons (45 ml) water and 1 tablespoon (8 g) flaxseed meal when substituting for eggs. When it comes to flax-seed meal, however, buyer beware. Many flaxseed meals on the market are the leftover by-products of the flaxseed oil extraction process. Unfortunately, this processing removes many of the healthy omega-3s of whole seeds. But fret not: You can make your own flaxseed meal by grinding seeds in a coffee grinder.

Chia seeds: Chia seeds are a great way to add a nice crunch to snacks such as granola. They are loaded with fiber, omega-3s, antioxidants, and protein. Further, because they absorb up to twelve times their own weight of liquid, chia seeds can help you feel full for prolonged periods. Plus, they serve as a thickener in things like pudding.

Pepitas (pumpkin seeds): These healthy seeds are a perfect snack, especially for anyone with anemia or low iron. And, just two ¼-cup (16 g) servings of pepitas have almost half the recommended daily amount of magnesium. Because approximately 70 percent of us are de-ficient in magnesium, this is a seed we could all use. Be sure to buy raw pepitas so you can manage the roasting process when you include them in snacks. You can also grind pepitas in a coffee grinder to make a flour perfect for baking nut-free, gluten-free, low-carb snacks.

Chocolate
Chocolate lovers, rejoice. Not only is chocolate loaded with antioxidants, which can help us age more gracefully, but it also has recently been show to be anti-inflammatory and to lower blood pressure. In addition, it raises serotonin levels, the feel-good hormone. Hallelujah!

Dark chocolate: While the processed sugar and milk found in most chocolate bars is not Paleo compliant, 100 percent dark chocolate is. You can add your own natural sweeteners to 100 percent cacao dark chocolate to re-create a milder, sweeter taste. In truth, I typically deviate from the rigidity of Paleo and use a chocolate with 70 percent cacao, which has a relatively low, and in my opinion, tolerable level of sugar. I've developed my recipes with 70 percent cacao in mind, so whether you enjoy the taste of 85 percent cacao or higher, or want to go as low as 60 percent cacao, you may need to adjust the amount of sweetener in the recipes that call for chocolate. As I learned in my own kitchen, taking notes and experimenting is half the fun!

Raw cacao: You can use raw cacao powder in place of dark chocolate. I choose raw cacao because it maintains nutrients that are typically destroyed during the high-heat phase of processed cocoa. Just be sure to add some extra sweetener if you are trying to replicate a particular recipe, as cacao is not naturally sweet. I like using cacao powder in drinks and other snacks because it is high in both magnesium and iron, and it is loaded with antioxidants. You can also use raw cacao nibs in place of chocolate chips, though the taste might be a bit bitter by comparison. Cacao does contain some caffeine, so if you are sensitive to it, be sure not to ingest a lot (say, more than 1 tablespoon, or 8 g) too late in the day or evening.

Carob: Carob is a great substitute for those who have dairy or chocolate allergies, or who are sensitive to caffeine. Like cacao, carob is made from a bean. Unlike raw cacao powder, however, carob is naturally sweet, so you may not need to use any additional sweeteners. If you are making a snack that is to be enjoyed later in the day or evening, and you are sensitive to caffeine, you may want to use carob instead of dark chocolate in a 1:1 ratio.

Natural Sweeteners

The ugly truth about sweeteners—even Paleo sweeteners—is that, for the most part, they are sugar. And sugar has an effect on our blood sugar levels, with spikes followed by crashes. Large swings in our blood sugar can, in the short term, impact our energy and concentration levels. Longer term, too much sugar can lead to inflammation and cause a host of associated issues ranging from diabetes to dementia. So, regardless of whether a sweetener is "Paleo" or processed, remember not to overdo it.

Of course, there are certainly better, more natural alternatives to using refined sugars. Because the highly processed refined sugars tend to have no nutritional value beyond empty calories, I prefer to use sweeteners that include antioxidants, vitamins, and minerals. I also shy away from sweeteners such as brown sugar and agave, which place a heavy burden on the liver and can cause degenerative health issues through inflammation. Most of the natural sweeteners I list below are burned by our bodies more efficiently, thereby placing less stress on our health.

Coconut palm sugar: This natural, unrefined sugar is produced from the sap of cut flower buds of the coconut palm. Similar in taste to brown sugar with a touch of caramel, it has the perfect amount of sweetness to be substituted for refined sugar using a 1:1 ratio. And most important, it has the same nutritional elements as coconut nectar (see below) and a low glycemic load with minimal impact on insulin or blood sugar levels. It is my favorite sweetener, and I use it for a majority of my recipes, as well as other recipes that call for refined sugar.

Coconut nectar: Coconut nectar comes from the sap of the coconut palm. This sap has a very low glycemic load and is an abundant source of minerals, seventeen amino acids, vitamin C, and B vitamins. I consider it the ideal liquid sweetener. To be honest, tasting it by itself may leave you skeptical. I certainly was at first. But after cooking with it for years, I have learned that it delivers the right amount of sweetness, and stickiness if needed. If you find that it doesn't suit your taste buds, use maple syrup or honey as a substitute—but it's worth trying, I promise! Shop around online for the best price.

Honey: Honey has many health benefits from its vitamins, amino acids, and small amount of minerals. It can help relieve cold or allergy symptoms, be used as an antibacterial, and, according to studies at the University of Memphis, it can increase endurance and stabilize blood sugar during exercise. I prefer to use a local, raw, dark honey, such as wildflower or buckwheat, as it is higher in antioxidants than the lighter honeys. Feel free to substitute honey with a lower-glycemic sweetener such as coconut nectar or coconut palm sugar in the recipes.

Maple syrup: Maple syrup is the boiled sap of maple trees. It is minimally processed and contains minerals such as manganese and zinc, which protect against viruses and keep our immune systems strong. The flavor of a good-quality maple syrup is undeniably delicious. While I love honey as an ingredient, it can sometimes leave a slight aftertaste that I don't always want or love. While maple flavor is superappealing, remember that it carries a higher glycemic load (like honey), so use it in moderation. I prefer to use grade B syrup, which is darker and is thought to contain more minerals than its grade A brother. I also enjoy its richer flavor.

Stevia: Stevia is a sweetener derived from the stevia plant. It is up to three hundred times sweeter than natural sugar, so a little goes a long way. I love to use a drop or two when a recipe needs just an extra touch of sweetness. Because stevia has a negligible effect on blood glucose, it does not raise insulin levels like other artificial sweeteners do. Just be sure you are getting 100 percent pure stevia. I like the liquid form because it tends to be of better quality and it is easier to regulate the amount you use. In baking, a little experimentation will be in order to achieve a desired level of sweetness, and, like coconut flour, it tends to dry out the finished product.

Fats

So many of us grew up with the misguided notion that eating fat was bad for us. Eating fat, we thought, would make us fat and sick. In fact, studies are showing that eating healthy fat (along with cutting carbs) does just the opposite. Healthy fats are essential to growth and development. In fact, DHA, a form of omega-3, along with cholesterol (found in coconut oil, eggs, and grass-fed beef), is a vital nutrient for growth, development, and maintenance of brain tissue.

But will eating fat make you fat? The short answer is no. As long as you aren't eating ten servings of nuts a day or coupling it with processed carbs, fat will not make you fat. Two-thirds of Americans are not overweight from eating healthy fats; rather, the issue stems from too many refined, processed carbs, sugar, and trans fats (the bad fat).

Healthy fats can actually help with weight management. In April 2014, six research studies showed that almonds can help improve satiety, reduce appetite, and may help reduce belly fat. Good thing there are plenty of recipes with almonds in this book!

Further, good fats can also protect us against many diseases because they can have an anti-inflammatory effect on our bodies. According to the Centers for Disease Control and Prevention (CDC), of the top ten causes of death in the United States, chronic, low-level inflammation contributes to at least seven. Anti-inflammatory omega-3s are found in foods including walnuts, chia seeds, flaxseeds, and wild salmon.

Moreover, these provide us with a great source of energy. The Paleo diet consists of healthy fats from nuts, seeds, avocados, olive oil, fish oil, and grass-fed meat, as well as some of my favorites below.

Coconut oil: With coconut oil being 92 percent saturated fat, it is great for brain development and growth. It also contains a high amount of medium-chain triglycerides, or MCTs, which, according to a researcher at Columbia University, means that the oil is used immediately for energy and less likely to be stored as fat. Further, according to Bruce Fife, ND, author of the *Coconut Oil Miracle*, coconut oil is antibacterial, antifungal, and antiviral. It can support your thyroid, heal your gut, and strengthen your immune system.

It is also the perfect nonstick coating when baking and panfrying because it does well with higher heat, and it won't go rancid quickly. If you are new to using coconut oil and looking to get one with a less "coconuty" flavor, try the unrefined Spectrum Naturals Brand as it has a very mild flavor. When choosing any coconut oil, choose unrefined, which means that the oils didn't lose any nutrients through a high-heat cycle of extraction.

Grass-fed butter: Technically this is a dairy product, and thus, not considered Paleo. But I will, on occasion, cook or bake with grass-fed butter, even though I don't typically eat dairy products such as cheeses, ice cream, and yogurts. Because the butter is grass-fed, it is loaded with vitamins A, D, and K, which are not typically found in butter produced from grain-fed cows. And because grass-fed butter is primarily fat (about 80 percent), meaning it has zero lactose (sugar) and less casein (protein) than other dairy products, it can be easier to digest for some people. If you prefer not to use any butter, you can always substitute ghee (if no dairy issues), palm shortening, or coconut oil.

Ghee: Clarified butter, which is free of both lactose and casein, is a great substitute for butter when it comes to cooking/sautéing and in most baked goods recipes. The smell and taste is absolutely amazing. It reminds me of a very robust butter. And, not only is it good for gut health, but it is also full of vitamins A, D, E, and K, which are important for bone, brain, heart, and immune system function.

Palm shortening: Made with organic palm oil, organic shortening is a healthy, dairy-free alternative to butter. So, anytime a recipe calls for butter or ghee, feel free to use this instead. It is vegan, virtually tasteless, and it bakes well and can make chewy cookies even chewier. My favorite brands (such as Spectrum Naturals and Tropical Traditions) are unrefined and not hydrogenated.

Paleo Milks

According to the American Dietetic Association, it is estimated that 75 percent of adults worldwide show some decrease in the ability to digest lactose as they age. Because the Paleo diet excludes foods that contain possible allergens, we need alternatives to dairy. Here are some of my favorites to use whether for cooking, baking, or even drinking.

Coconut milk: When cooking, baking, or making smoothies, I use only canned coconut milk, which comes in both full-fat and light varieties. I use brands that contain only coconut, water, and sometimes guar gum, and that use BPA-free cans. Coconut milk that comes in the carton is often diluted and formulated for drinking. I use full-fat coconut milk for baking and cooking most of the time. It is full of healthy saturated fats that are nourishing for the brain, and the fat adds a nice creamy texture to whatever I'm making. The only time I use light coconut milk is when making smoothies because it has a less potent coconut flavor. I look for brands that contain only coconut milk and water.

Almond milk: There are many varieties of almond milk on the market, and knowing how to choose the right one can be confusing. Some are very high in sugar, so be aware. I use unsweetened almond milk with zero grams of sugar or the "original" version with 7 grams of sugar or less. Also make sure your milk is free of carrageenan, an emulsifier and thickener that has been linked to stomach problems and inflammation, especially if you have any type of gastrointestinal disease.

Additional Supplies

By now you've probably noticed a lot of organic and "purer" ingredients. Yes, buying organic foods and grass-fed beef is more expensive, but I've found a few ways to lessen the burden. For example, we have started to buy our meat in bulk at a local farmers' market. When it comes to fruit, we do not go organic on everything, such as thick-skin produce including watermelons, bananas, and avocados. Also, there are many great online resources for getting items such as nut flours and sweeteners at a better price. And, even some larger-box, discount retailers now have many great organic products such as eggs, spinach, wild blueberries, and coconut oil, to name a few.

Meats: Meat is a fantastic source of protein and fat. With the invention of hormones to increase growth rate or production in animals, and the antibiotics that are sure to follow, be sure to opt for organic meats. Also, in order to get the most humanely raised and healthiest meats, opt for grass-fed when available.

Organic eggs: To my mind, pasture-raised eggs are the clear winner in terms of nutrients and taste (see "Cracking the Egg Confusion," page 30), but they can also be pricey. I try to use free-range when possible, but I really just try to get eggs from chickens that weren't loaded with hormones and antibiotics. When Paleo baking, set out your eggs so they can warm to room temperature because often they are being mixed with liquids that need to stay liquid or soft, such as butter or coconut oil.

Celtic sea salt: Celtic sea salt is my favorite salt not only because it tastes divine, but also because it supplies our bodies with more than eighty trace minerals and elements that other refined salts don't provide. While there are salts that are more reasonably priced, I recommend that you choose a salt with some color (gray like Celtic or pink like Himalayan) to ensure that the minerals have not been refined or bleached out of it. You can use 1:1 for any salts in these recipes.

Baking soda: Although baking soda and baking powder are both leavening agents that help baked goods rise, I prefer to use baking soda because baking powder tends to contain more additives such as cornstarch, whereas baking soda is just sodium bicarbonate.

Cracking the Egg Confusion

Free-range? Cage-free? What about organic-cage-free? With so many choices, it can all be very confusing. Here's a list to help you decide on the best eggs for your money. Note that unless a carton says "no antibiotics" or "GMO-free," etc., it doesn't mean the eggs are free of antibiotics, hormones, vaccines, or feed that may include animal by-products or GMO-crops. Unless it says "NO _____," you have to assume it's in there.

Cage-free: Chickens are not raised in small cages, although it doesn't mean the hens have access to the outdoors or that they have not been raised in tight conditions, in a barnlike setting, with clipped beaks and wings, and very little exposure to sunlight.

Free-range: Chickens have some exposure to the outdoors for a portion of their lives, but there are no absolute standards on duration spent outdoors or the quality or size of their outside roaming area.

Omega-3 enriched: Feed given to the chickens is enriched with an omega-3 diet, usually in the form of flaxseeds, which is a great way to get in extra nutrients. Just make sure the chickens are also hormone- and antibiotic-free.

Organic vegetarian-fed: Chickens are not fed any meat or fish (since when do chickens eat cows or salmon?), but rather an organic vegetarian-based diet. While this might sound "healthier," chickens are not meant to be vegetarian (see Pasture-raised, below).

Certified organic: The feed that is given to these chickens is organic, and the chickens are not given antibiotics or hormones. These chickens most likely have some (not all) exposure to sunlight, but "organic" does not mean they are free-range or pasture-raised.

Pasture-raised: These chickens are free to roam on open grassland, eat an organic diet, enjoy bugs and worms, see daylight, and are not given any hormones or antibiotics. While this is clearly the most humane way to raise the hens, they also provide us with eggs that have darker, richer yolks that taste better and have a higher nutritional value. A 2007 study by *Mother Earth News* showed that pastured eggs have, in comparison to those laid by hens confined to a cage:

- 66 percent more vitamin A
- two times more omega-3 fatty acids
- three times more vitamin E
- seven times more beta-carotene

While they are more expensive (find a friend with chickens!), they are worth it. If you can't always get the pasture-raised, then at least try to go organic to ensure that they are free of hormones and antibiotics.

Unsweetened shredded coconut: Buy shredded coconut without added sugar. Also make sure that it does not say "low fat." The only ingredient in shredded coconut should be coconut.

Gelatin: Gelatin is made from the connective tissues of animals, a great source of collagen, protein, and amino acids, all of which benefit hair, skin, nails, digestion, immune function, and joint mobility, as well as reducing cellulite and inflammation. Unlike the Technicolor-hued, sugar-laden powders that come in colorful boxes, gelatin is flavorless, so it is a great addition to smoothies or hot drinks for a nutritional boost. But the real fun is using gelatin to give that specific texture to certain snacks like Strawberry Gummies (page 120). Two higher-quality, less-refined brands of gelatin are Bernard Jensen and Great Lakes Gelatin, both made from grass-fed cows and available online.

Organic tamari or coconut aminos: Tamari is a gluten-free organic soy sauce that adds the right amount of umami to most dishes. If you have an allergy to soy, an autoimmune or a thyroid condition, or just follow a strict Paleo protocol, use coconut aminos (a soy-free seasoning sauce made from coconut tree sap that also has less sodium than soy sauce).

Nutritional yeast: Nutritional yeast is an inactive yeast, grown on molasses and then harvested, washed, and dried with heat. Because it's inactive, it doesn't grow like baking yeast does, so it is typically Candida-free and is generally safe for individuals who have sensitivities to other types of yeast. It is a great source of protein and rich in many vitamins (especially the Bs), minerals, and amino acids. The nutty and cheesy flavor makes it a great cheese substitute for vegans or people who don't consume dairy. But in our household, it's a requirement on the Easy "Cheesy" Kale Chips (page 76). My kids love this stuff and will eat it by the spoonful!

Psyllium husk powder: While it may sound odd to use psyllium husk powder, which is sometimes used for regularity because of its fiber, it's great for giving gluten-free baked goods that spongy, almost gluten-like feel. You are only typically using a small amount per recipe, such as a tablespoon or two, and because it's a water-soluble, natural fiber, it can add healthy bulk to the diet.

Kitchen Equipment

What follows is a quick list of some of my favorite kitchen items. While none of these is necessary to make any of the recipes in this book, they certainly have helped me save significant prep time.

Immersion blender: Sure you can use a standard blender, but you can really cut to the chase with an immersion blender. It is especially helpful with puréed soups (no transferring of hot liquids) and smoothies (single servings). You don't have to spend a lot of money (under $20), they are easy to clean, and they don't take up much kitchen space.

High-power blender: Any blender can certainly help speed the mixing process, but high-power blenders such as a Vitamix, Ninja, or Blendtec, have the amazing ability to liquefy almost anything, including kale. They are also great at making soups creamy and silky. Though these blenders are pricey, your soups will truly taste like they came from a restaurant.

Food processor: Ever watch one of those cooking shows and just ogle how quickly experienced chefs can chop veggies? Amazing. It seems to take me forever to slice anything, so I cheat with my handy-dandy food processor. It slices. It dices. And it saves a ton of time. My $40 food processor has stood the test of time.

Mandolin slicer: Because my family makes so many sweet potato fries and squash chips, this is my all-time favorite kitchen tool. It is very quick and easy to use, and it produces uniform slices so your veggies cook evenly. But please be careful! If you aren't paying attention you can really cut yourself. I got mine online for $20. Best investment, ever.

Silicone cupcake liners: One of my least favorite things to clean in the kitchen is a dirty muffin pan. Getting bits of baked-on whatever out of the crevices is enough to drive a person crazy. These silicone cupcake liners have saved my time and my sanity. And the muffins (especially the egg ones) slide out so easily. You can get a set of twelve online for about $7.

Parchment paper: My second-least favorite thing to clean is a dirty baking sheet. Parchment paper to the rescue. It also comes in handy when you need to flatten doughy balls into cookies.

A Key to Allergen-Free Recipes

While all of the recipes in this book are gluten-free, and chapter 6 is specifically for nut-free snacks, there are many other nut-free, egg-free, and dairy-free recipes. This key will help make it easier for you to quickly spot whether a recipe is free of these ingredients:

 nuts

 eggs

 dairy

Some recipes denote "dairy-free," even though they contain chocolate chips. If you have a dairy allergy or sensitivity, substitute the chocolate with carob chips or Enjoy Life brand of chocolate chips, which are dairy-free (as well as gluten-free, nut-free, and soy-free). For those recipes that call for a single pat of butter, you can easily substitute it with coconut oil, palm shortening, or even ghee (if you know you can tolerate it), but those recipes are not called "dairy-free."

Also, note that some recipes that are not marked "nut-free" may be made so by substituting sunflower seed butter for the almond or cashew butter. So, while the recipes in chapter 6 are truly nut-free, there may be other recipes scattered throughout the remaining chapters that can easily be transformed into safe nut-free options, even though they're not marked as such.

SCHOOL AND WORK SNACKS

Nourishing Snacks to Keep You Focused and Full All Day Long

Ten years ago, if you asked someone about their ideal snack at work, the answer would likely have been, "Whatever comes out of the vending machine." While fig bars or corn chips are certainly convenient and (some might say) tasty, these sort of sugary, salty, high-carbohydrate, processed foods are remarkably rough on the body, and, even worse, the mind.

Sadly, snack time at school isn't much better. Fishy-shaped crackers, high-fructose "fruit" strips, and processed cookies are all actively working against our children's ability to concentrate.

Study after study has shown that consuming high-carbohydrate, high-glycemic foods spikes insulin, leading to a postmeal crash in both energy and focus. Ever wonder why you want to take a nap about an hour after a slice of pizza?

Fortunately, science is homing in on how our food can help us focus.

You may have heard about the importance of protein in our diet, but only recently have we come to understand what a huge role high-protein foods play in our mental health. Studies show that protein improves concentration levels. It elevates dopamine, which regulates happiness, and neurotransmitters that help brain cells "talk" with each other and function properly. Research also suggests that high-protein diets may reduce symptoms of ADHD and improve behavior and attention.

By consuming snacks that include beneficial fatty acids like omega-3s, which are crucial to a well-functioning brain, concentration can be improved. Because omega 3-s can't be produced by the body, it is important to get them from our diet—walnuts and flaxseeds are great options. One particular type of omega-3 is DHA, which has been shown in some studies to have a direct impact on ADHD and concentration levels.

Likewise, it is hard to stay focused at work or school if your tummy is rumbling. Snacks with a healthy amount of fiber can help you stay satiated for extended periods. Fiber comes in two forms: soluble and insoluble. While insoluble fiber passes through the digestive system relatively untouched, soluble fiber, the kind found in nuts, flaxseeds, and psyllium husk, absorbs water in your stomach and gut, thereby helping you feel full longer.

In this chapter, I've pulled together recipes that, by balancing fiber and protein, are optimized for heightened concentration, a consistent level of energy, and staving off hunger in order to help you be the best you and your children can be at work or school. In addition to being super-healthy, most of these snacks are nut-free, which makes them nice options in "peanut/nut-free" schools.

 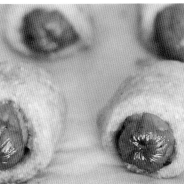 

SAVORY BAKED CHICKEN NUGGETS

Chicken nuggets are always a favorite with the kids, but you know you love them, too! They are supertasty and an excellent source of protein to help keep that concentration level up all day. I like to make a double batch of these and store them in the freezer in an airtight bag or container. Just be sure to put them in a container in the fridge for school or work the night before, so they will be ready for afternoon snack time the next day. Sometimes I also make a big batch and keep the uncooked chicken pieces with the "flour" mixture in a freezer bag and just take out and bake as needed.

¼ cup (55 g) grass-fed butter, melted

1 cup (100 g) almond meal or cashew flour

3 tablespoons (24 g) sesame seeds

1 tablespoon (7 g) paprika

2 teaspoons (5 g) onion powder

1½ teaspoons (9 g) sea salt

1 teaspoon garlic powder

¼ teaspoon cayenne pepper

1 pound (455 g) chicken breasts (about 3 large breasts), cut into bite-size pieces

Preheat the oven to 400°F (200°C, or gas mark 6). Place a wire rack in a baking sheet or baking dish. (If you don't have a wire rack, line the baking sheet with parchment paper.)

Place the melted butter in a small bowl. In a separate small bowl, mix together the almond meal, sesame seeds, paprika, onion powder, salt, garlic powder, and cayenne pepper.

Put 5 or so pieces of chicken in the bowl with the butter and coat them well. Then put the chicken into the bowl with the spices and coat evenly. Set the chicken on the wire rack or parchment paper and repeat the process until all of your chicken is coated.

Bake for 10 minutes. Then turn the oven to broil, and bake another 4 or 5 minutes, until golden brown. You don't have to flip them (thank goodness, because it's a pain!).

Nuggets store well in the fridge for 3 to 4 days or in the freezer for up to 6 months.

YIELD: about 24 nuggets

BACON & EGG MAPLE MUFFINS

With a sweet hint of maple and some salty bacon, this delectable snack is superfilling and satisfying—no matter the time of day. And because it's made with an abundance of eggs, considered "brain food" by David Perlmutter, M.D., in his bestselling book *Grain Brain*, this muffin clearly is an ideal snack.

8 to 10 slices nitrate-free bacon

7 eggs, at room temperature

¼ cup (55 g) grass-fed butter, melted

¼ cup (60 ml) unsweetened canned coconut milk (stirred first)

2 tablespoons (40 g) maple syrup

½ cup (56 g) coconut flour

½ teaspoon sea salt

¼ teaspoon baking soda

Preheat the oven to 400°F (200°C, or gas mark 6). Place the bacon on a foil-lined baking sheet and bake for 8 to 10 minutes on each side. You want it to get really brown and crispy!

While the bacon bakes, mix together the eggs, butter, coconut milk, and maple syrup in a medium bowl. In a small bowl, mix together the coconut flour, salt, and baking soda. Add to the egg mixture and stir well. Make sure you get all of the clumps out from the coconut flour.

When the bacon is done, place it on a paper towel to cool off a bit and then crumble it into the batter.

Reduce the heat to 350°F (180°C, or gas mark 4). Line a 12-cup muffin pan with silicone or paper muffin liners, or grease the cups. Fill the cups about two-thirds full. Bake for 20 minutes, or until a toothpick inserted in the middle of a muffin comes out clean.

These freeze well. Just pull one out the night before and place it in the fridge so it will be ready to go to school/work the next day. They're best when reheated but also good when eaten cool or at room temperature.

YIELD: 12 muffins

PIGS IN A BLANKET

These protein-filled, fun little snacks will be devoured by even the finickiest eater. Just be sure not to eat them all at once so that you'll actually have some snacks to take to work or send to school!

¾ cup (84 g) almond flour

¼ cup (32 g) arrowroot powder

2 tablespoons (16 g) psyllium husk powder

Pinch of sea salt

½ cup (120 ml) unsweetened canned light coconut milk

½ cup (120 ml) water

24 cocktail pork franks (such as Applegate's The Greatest Little Organic Cocktail Pork Franks) or 12 organic grass-fed (Applegate) hot dogs (cut in half)

1 tablespoon (14 g) grass-fed butter, melted

Preheat the oven to 375°F (190°C, or gas mark 5). Line a baking sheet with parchment paper.

In a medium bowl, mix together the almond flour, arrowroot, psyllium husk powder, and salt. Then stir in the coconut milk. In a small pan, bring the water to a boil. As soon as it boils, pour the water into the mixture and stir everything together until a dough forms.

Get out two large pieces of parchment paper (each almost big enough to cover a cutting board). Place the dough on one piece of parchment paper and then place the other piece of paper on top of the dough. Use your hands, on top of the paper, to squish the dough down like pizza dough. Then use a rolling pin to flatten the dough into a large rectangle, about ¼-inch (6 mm) thick.

With a pizza cutter, cut a line across the middle of the dough. Then cut triangle shapes along the top and bottom halves. The bottom (the widest part) of each triangle should be about 1 inch (2.5 cm) wide. Set a frank on the bottom of a triangle, and then roll it all the way to the point. Place it on the prepared baking sheet, point-side down. Repeat with the remaining dough and franks.

Bake for about 8 minutes. Brush melted butter on top of the dough, then return to the oven for 12 to 13 minutes, or until the dough starts to brown and is light and crispy like a croissant. Let cool briefly before eating. Store in the fridge for 3 days or the freezer for 3 months. When reheating them, you may want to toast them in a 350°F (180°C, or gas mark 4) oven or toaster oven for best results.

YIELD: 24 piggies

BACON CAULIFLOWER SOUP

My whole family loves this restaurant-quality soup. And, because cauliflower has choline, a B vitamin that is essential for your brain's neurotransmitters and can help with focus, it is a great snack during the school or work day. Keep it in a warmed thermos (run under hot water for a couple of minutes in the morning before you leave) for a great snack that will warm both your body and your mind!

6 to 8 slices nitrate-free bacon

1 small yellow onion, roughly chopped

2 cloves garlic, minced

1 large or 2 small heads cauliflower, roughly chopped

1 quart (946 ml) lower-sodium chicken broth, or as needed

1 tablespoon (18 g) sea salt

1 teaspoon black pepper

2/3 cup (160 ml) unsweetened canned light coconut milk

Cut the bacon into pieces (about 4 or 5 pieces per slice, but slice it all together to save time). Put it in a large pot and cook over medium-high heat until it starts to get crispy. Add the onion and garlic, and sauté for a couple of minutes until they start to brown. Continuously stir so the bacon doesn't burn and the onion and garlic cook on all sides.

Add the cauliflower, chicken broth (fill it so it covers the cauliflower by about 2 inches, or 5 cm), salt, and pepper to the pot. Bring to a boil, then turn the heat down to low and cover with the lid. Cook until the cauliflower starts to become soft, about 10 minutes.

Stir in the coconut milk, then carefully transfer to a high-speed blender (in batches, if necessary). You can also use an immersion blender, which is easier and less messy, but you won't get quite as creamy and fluffy a result. Blend on high for 60 to 90 seconds, until creamy and very smooth. Return to the pot and heat through.

Enjoy with some spicy sausage, chives, more bacon, cheese, or whatever you prefer. Or just enjoy it as is. It's good any way!

When storing soup in a plastic container, make sure the soup is cool and the container is BPA-free.

YIELD: 5 quarts (4.7 L)

HOMEMADE BEEF JERKY

Beef jerky is a great and easy way to get a lot of protein. But unfortunately, most jerkys available in grocery stores are made with meats containing hormones and antibiotics. In addition, the jerkys are typically full of sugar, gluten/wheat, and unhealthy preservatives. I was reluctant to make jerky because I thought it might be difficult, but it turns out it is incredibly easy and only requires a little prep work. It's so worth it!

2½ pounds (1135 g) grass-fed London broil (flank steak or any lean meat)

1 cup (235 ml) gluten-free tamari soy sauce or coconut aminos

1 tablespoon (20 g) dark raw honey

2 teaspoons (5 g) onion powder

1 teaspoon garlic powder

1 teaspoon sea salt

Place the meat in the freezer for 1 to 2 hours to make it easier to slice. Remove from the freezer and trim off any visible fat. Then slice it against the grain into thin strips (about ¼ inch [65 mm] thick).

In a plastic freezer bag, combine the soy sauce, honey, onion powder, garlic powder, and salt. Add the meat and marinate for at least 4 hours, preferably overnight.

Preheat the oven to 170°F (76°C), if you aren't using a dehydrator. On a parchment-lined baking sheet, lay the meat out flat, but make sure none of it is touching or overlapping.

Cook for 4 to 6 hours (it will depend on the thickness), until the desired texture is reached. Flip the meat once or twice while cooking. If using a dehydrator, allow it to dehydrate for 4 to 5 hours.

Store the jerky in the fridge or freezer, but it is fine to keep at room temperature for a couple of days. Ours usually doesn't last that long around here, though.

YIELD: 20 to 25 pieces

SUN-DRIED TOMATO CHICKEN SLIDERS

This flavorful slider is a fun alternative to a traditional chicken burger. And because it's all protein, it's a great snack to keep your concentration going strong.

1 pound (455 g) ground chicken

½ small onion, finely chopped

2 tablespoons (14 g) chopped sun-dried tomatoes packed in oil

2 tablespoons (5 g) chopped fresh basil

2 cloves garlic, pressed

2 teaspoons (12 g) sea salt

1 teaspoon black pepper

2 tablespoons (27 g) coconut oil

In a medium bowl, combine the chicken, onion, sun-dried tomatoes, basil, garlic, salt, and pepper until well combined. To form sliders, take a spoonful of mixture and shape a patty that is 2 to 3 inches (5 to 7.5 cm) in diameter.

Heat a large pan over medium-high and add the coconut oil. Carefully place the patties in the pan, as many as you can without touching. Once the patties start to brown, carefully turn them, and cook for a few more minutes so they can brown. Then turn the heat down to low and cook for about 7 more minutes, or until no longer pink in the middle. Snack on them as is, or turn them into a meal by using them to top a salad.

YIELD: about 15 sliders

CAULIFLOWER PIZZA BITES

This is my favorite gluten-free pizza crust turned into small, easy-to-eat pizzas. I know it sounds odd, but you just have to try it to see for yourself! It just so happens that this is the healthiest pizza crust around. With six different types of B vitamins for energy, lots of vitamin C, and a load of antioxidants, this is a super snack.

1 large head cauliflower, cored and broken into large florets

1 egg

4 ounces (115 g) soft goat cheese (chèvre)

1 tablespoon (3 g) dried oregano

1 teaspoon sea salt

Optional toppings:

    Tomato or pizza sauce

    Parmesan or mozzarella cheese

    Olives, pepperoni, etc.

Preheat the oven to 400°F (200°C, or gas mark 6). Grease 12 cups of a mini-muffin pan.

In a food processor, chop up the cauliflower until it is a rice-like consistency. Bring a pot of water to a boil. Add the cauliflower and cook for 6 to 8 minutes, until soft. Strain and rinse with cold water. Lay out a clean kitchen towel. Pour the "rice" onto the towel, wrap the towel around the "rice," and twist it and squeeze out as much water as you can.

In a medium bowl, beat the egg and add the goat cheese, oregano, and salt. Add the cauliflower "rice" and blend it all together with your hands. It's messy, but it works best this way.

Evenly spoon the mixture into the muffin cups, filling them close to the top. Press down the dough evenly and firmly to ensure it sticks together. Bake for 15 to 18 minutes, or until the tops start to turn a light brown. Remove from the oven and let cool in the pan for at least 10 minutes.

Dip in tomato sauce or add whatever toppings you desire.

YIELD: 12 pizza bites

CHICKEN MAPLE SAUSAGE MEATBALLS

Studies show that protein helps with concentration, and these easy-to-eat, kid- and adult-friendly mini meatballs are an easy way to get more protein into our bodies. To make these nut-free, substitute 1 tablespoon (7 g) coconut flour for the almond meal.

1 pound (455 g) hormone-free ground chicken

1 egg

2 tablespoons (12 g) almond meal

1 tablespoon (20 g) maple syrup

1 teaspoon sea salt

1 teaspoon garlic powder

1 teaspoon paprika

1 teaspoon Dijon mustard

½ teaspoon dried rosemary

½ teaspoon dried thyme

Preheat the oven to 400°F (200°C, or gas mark 6). Line a baking sheet with parchment paper.

In a medium bowl, combine the chicken, egg, almond meal, maple syrup, salt, garlic powder, paprika, mustard, rosemary, and thyme. With your hands, make golf ball–size balls out of the mixture and lay on the prepared baking sheet. Bake for 18 to 20 minutes, until cooked through.

YIELD: about 15 meatballs

TIP: For kids, add toothpicks to the meatballs. Toothpicks can make food more fun for little ones.

MEDITERRANEAN BREAD

Just like a trip back to Greece (or even just a Greek restaurant), this scrumptious bread will keep your taste buds happy and keep you full for hours. And with antioxidants from the artichokes, olives, and sun-dried tomatoes, lots of omega-3s from the flax, and other healthy fats, this is the tastiest anti-inflammatory snack out there.

1 cup (112 g) almond flour

1 cup (128 g) ground flaxseed meal

½ cup (56 g) coconut flour

1 tablespoon (8 g) arrowroot powder

1 teaspoon sea salt

1 teaspoon dried crushed rosemary

¾ teaspoon baking soda

½ teaspoon dried oregano

½ teaspoon dried basil

5 eggs, at room temperature

1 cup (235 ml) unsweetened canned coconut milk (stirred first)

⅓ cup (75 g) grass-fed butter, melted

1 tablespoon (15 ml) apple cider vinegar

½ cup (150 g) marinated artichoke hearts, chopped

¼ cup (28 g) chopped sun-dried tomatoes in olive oil

¼ cup (25 g) pitted and sliced Kalamata or black olives

Preheat the oven to 350°F (180°C, or gas mark 4). Grease a 5 x 9-inch (13 x 23 cm) loaf pan with olive oil.

In a large bowl, combine the almond flour, flaxseed meal, coconut flour, arrowroot, salt, rosemary, baking soda, oregano, and basil. Make sure there are no lumps. Add the eggs, coconut milk, melted butter, and apple cider vinegar and stir until combined. Fold in the artichoke hearts, sun-dried tomatoes, and olives. Spread the batter into the prepared loaf pan and bake for about 50 minutes, until a toothpick inserted in the middle comes out clean. Allow to cool for 20 minutes before slicing and serving, alone or dipped in marinara sauce. You can also store it for up to 5 days in the fridge.

YIELD: 8 servings

EGG MUFFINS

Who says eggs are just for breakfast? Eggs are a fabulous source of protein as well as choline, which is both vital for normal cognitive development and helps protect our liver. These snacks are a much more fun, on-the-go egg alternative to the traditional hard-boiled egg. And you can spice these up with any other ingredients you enjoy! Adjust the amounts to suit your taste.

½ pound (225 g) ground sausage (or remove from casing)

4 ounces (115 g) mushrooms, chopped

1 tablespoon (14 g) grass-fed butter

10 eggs

2 handfuls of spinach

⅓ cup (38 g) shredded Cheddar cheese (optional)

1 teaspoon sea salt

Dash of black pepper

Add-ins:
Ham, artichoke hearts, sun-dried tomatoes, hot sauce, etc. (get creative!)

Preheat the oven to 350°F (180°C, or gas mark 4). Line a 12-cup muffin pan with silicone muffin liners (this will help a ton) or grease the pan well with palm shortening or coconut oil.

In a large skillet over medium heat, cook the sausage until no longer pink, about 8 minutes. Remove from the skillet and set aside. Sauté the mushrooms or any other veggies you use in butter for a few minutes until they become soft.

In a medium bowl, beat the eggs, and then add in the raw spinach, cooked vegetables, and cheese, if using. Season with salt, pepper, and other seasonings as desired.

Pour the egg mixture into the muffin cups about halfway full. Bake for about 20 minutes, until they rise and start to brown on top. Remove from the oven and allow to cool for 10 minutes. If you didn't use silicone muffin liners, run a butter knife along the edges of the muffins before removing. Serve immediately or store in the fridge for up to 3 days or freezer for 3 months. Pack one up before heading out for the day.

YIELD: 12 muffins

MEXICAN MUFFINS

Who doesn't love tacos? Now you can have them any time you want! Studies show that grass-fed beef can help boost brain development, process, and function; help control ADHD symptoms; and also help with learning disabilities. So what better way to get this portable snack in your busy day when focus is of the utmost importance?

1 pound (455 g) grass-fed ground beef

1 egg

2 teaspoons (5 g) ground cumin

1 teaspoon chili powder

1 teaspoon sea salt

½ teaspoon ground black pepper

¾ cup (195 g) thick and chunky salsa (optional)

½ cup (58 g) grated sharp Cheddar cheese

Preheat the oven to 350°F (180°C, or gas mark 4). Grease a 12-cup muffin pan.

In a medium bowl, combine the beef, egg, cumin, chili powder, salt, and pepper by hand. Spoon the mixture into the prepared muffin pan. Top each "muffin" with salsa, if desired, and cheese. Bake for 20 to 25 minutes, or until desired doneness. Cool for 10 minutes. You may want to pull out each muffin as soon as they cool a bit and place them on a paper towel because they will be pretty wet when they come out of the oven.

YIELD: 12 muffins

TERIYAKI SALMON CAKES

Salmon is one of the healthiest foods on the planet, and while these omega-3–filled cakes are a great way to reduce inflammation, jet fuel your brain, and provide long-lasting energy with lots of B vitamins, they also taste amazing. And they are easy to eat with your hands, warm or cold, in a salad, or however you would prefer.

2 cans (8 ounces [225 g] each) wild salmon

3 eggs

½ cup (56 g) almond flour/ meal

½ cup (4 g) fresh cilantro, chopped

2 scallions (white parts only), chopped

2 tablespoons (28 ml) tamari (gluten-free soy) or coconut aminos

1 tablespoon (15 ml) lemon juice

1 tablespoon (8 g) fresh grated ginger

1 teaspoon onion powder

1 teaspoon garlic powder

¾ teaspoon sea salt

¾ teaspoon black pepper

2 to 3 tablespoons (28 to 45 ml) sesame or coconut oil

Place the salmon in a medium bowl. Remove the skin and bones from the fish, if necessary. Add the eggs, almond flour, cilantro, scallions, tamari, lemon juice, ginger, onion powder, garlic powder, salt, and pepper and mix together with your hands. Form the mixture into 8 patties, about 2½ inches (6.5 cm) in diameter.

In a large skillet over medium-high heat, add about 1 tablespoon (15 ml) of the sesame oil. Place a few of the patties in the skillet, being careful not to overlap them. Cook for 4 to 5 minutes, until the edges are brown, and then carefully turn each with a spatula. Cook for about 4 more minutes, until cooked through. Repeat with the remaining oil and patties.

YIELD: 8 cakes

BUFFALO CHICKEN WINGS

Ready for a little spice? Traditional buffalo wings are delicious, but too often they are fried in unhealthy oils and coated with gluten. This wonderful recipe is a Paleo twist on a favorite party snack that can be enjoyed anywhere, anytime for a protein-packed snack.

2¾ pounds (1245 g) raw chicken wings

½ cup (64 g) arrowroot powder

1 teaspoon sea salt

½ teaspoon garlic powder

½ teaspoon cayenne pepper (optional)

½ cup (112 g) grass-fed butter

½ cup gluten-free hot sauce (such as Texas Pete's)

Set the wings on a few paper towels and pat dry. In a resealable plastic freezer bag, combine the arrowroot, salt, garlic powder, and cayenne (if using). Add the wings to the bag, and shake until they are well coated. Set a wire rack on a baking sheet, and place the wings on the rack. Put the pan in the fridge for 1 hour to help the wings absorb the spices and dry out so they won't end up soggy.

Preheat the oven to 400°F (200°C, or gas mark 6).

After the hour of refrigeration, bake the wings for 20 minutes. Turn the wings over and bake for another 20 minutes.

While the wings bake, in a small saucepan, melt the butter and stir in the hot sauce until well combined. Set aside. As it sits, it will thicken up, which will add more flavor to the wings.

Take the wings out of the oven and brush them with the sauce. Return to the oven and bake for an additional 10 minutes. Broil them for the last minute or two to get them crispy.

YIELD: about 2 dozen wings

ITALIAN MEATBALLS

Not only does grass-fed meat contain lots of iron, but it also has many powerful nutrients that help build strong bones and a strong immune system. It also provides a good source of steady energy and concentration, and on top of that, it burns belly fat from its abundant CLA (conjugated linoleic acid), a fatty acid. You heard me right! Talk about a perfect snack. And these absolutely delicious meatballs don't need any messy tomato sauce, which makes them perfect for packing.

1 pound (455 g) grass-fed ground beef

½ pound (225 g) ground Italian sausage (removed from casing if needed)

½ small onion, finely chopped or grated

2 eggs

2 cloves garlic, minced

¼ cup (28 g) almond meal or flour

3 tablespoons (12 g) fresh parsley, finely chopped

1½ teaspoons (9 g) sea salt

1 teaspoon ground black pepper

1 teaspoon dried basil

1 teaspoon dried oregano

Preheat the oven to 350°F (180°C, or gas mark 4).

In a medium bowl, mix together the beef, sausage, onion, eggs, garlic, almond meal, parsley, salt, pepper, basil, and oregano by hand. Form into meatballs about 3 inches (7.5 cm) in diameter.

Add the meatballs to a large cast-iron skillet (or other ovenproof skillet) over medium-high heat. Cook until they are browned on all sides. Then place the skillet in the oven (or transfer the meatballs to a baking sheet) and bake for an additional 10 minutes.

YIELD: about 15 meatballs

APPLE CRUMB BITES

With just a touch of sweetness, this bite-size snack really hits the spot. And with a whole cup of walnuts, which have the highest amount of omega-3s of any nut, and coconut, which has fat to fuel the brain, they can really help recharge your mind and keep your focus strong.

2 large apples, chopped

1 cup (145 g) raw almonds

1 cup (120 g) raw walnuts

1 cup (80 g) unsweetened shredded coconut

2 tablespoons (24 g) coconut palm sugar

1 tablespoon (7 g) cinnamon

½ teaspoon sea salt

3 eggs

1 tablespoon (15 ml) vanilla extract

1 tablespoon (14 g) grass-fed butter, melted

Preheat the oven to 350°F (180°C, or gas mark 4). Line a baking sheet with parchment paper.

In a food processor, blend the apples, almonds, walnuts, coconut, coconut palm sugar, cinnamon, and salt until the apples and nuts are chopped into small pieces. In a medium bowl, combine the eggs, vanilla, and butter. Add the nut/apple mixture to the bowl and stir well. Use a tablespoon to scoop the mixture onto the prepared baking sheet and flatten just slightly with your hand to shape. Bake for about 30 minutes, or until lightly browned along the edges.

YIELD: about 30 bites

SUPERSMART BARS

These taste like candy bars! But with the omega-3–rich walnuts, which can help with concentration, and the magnesium-packed cashews, which can help improve memory, this is the exact opposite of a candy bar. Further, the low-glycemic coconut nectar can help stabilize blood sugar levels, while the dark chocolate offers a little mental boost. This is an ideal snack for school or work!

1 cup (120 g) walnuts

1 cup (110 g) cashews

1 cup (80 g) unsweetened shredded coconut

2/3 cup (175 g) almond butter

1/3 cup (72 g) coconut oil, melted

1/3 cup (115 g) coconut nectar

1 tablespoon (15 ml) vanilla extract

1/2 teaspoon sea salt

1/3 cup (58 g) dark chocolate chips

In a food processor, blend the walnuts, cashews, coconut, almond butter, coconut oil, coconut nectar, vanilla, and salt until the mixture starts to solidify. Then place the mixture into an 8 × 8-inch (20 × 20 cm) baking dish or pan and press firmly until flat and even. Place in the fridge for 30 to 60 minutes.

Set a small mixing bowl over a small pot of simmering water (be careful that the bowl does not touch the water). Put the chocolate chips in the bowl and stir until melted. Spread the chocolate over the bars and put back in the fridge until it hardens. Cut into 2 × 2-inch (5 × 5 cm) squares. You may want to use a metal spatula to get the squares out. The first one may be tricky to get out but the rest are easy. Store in the fridge for up to a week.

YIELD: 16 bars

CINNAMON BLUEBERRY BREAD

Studies show that diets rich in blueberries can significantly improve both learning capacity and motor skills. So, with a full cup of blueberries in this protein-rich, fiber-filled, and omega-3–fortified bread, you can be sure you'll be ready to focus on any task at hand.

- ¾ cup (84 g) coconut flour
- ¼ cup (32 g) ground flaxseed meal
- 1 tablespoon plus 1 teaspoon (10 g) ground cinnamon
- 1 tablespoon (8 g) psyllium husk powder
- ½ teaspoon baking soda
- ¼ teaspoon sea salt
- 7 eggs
- ½ cup (170 g) maple syrup
- ⅓ cup (75 g) grass-fed butter, melted, or ghee
- 2 tablespoons (28 ml) unsweetened canned coconut milk (stirred first)
- 1 tablespoon (15 ml) vanilla extract
- 1 teaspoon apple cider vinegar
- 1 cup (145 g) organic blueberries

Preheat the oven to 350°F (180°C, or gas mark 4). Grease a 5 x 9-inch (13 x 23 cm) loaf pan.

In a small bowl, mix together the coconut flour, flaxseed meal, cinnamon, psyllium husk powder, baking soda, and salt. In a medium bowl, whisk together the eggs, maple syrup, melted butter, coconut milk, vanilla, and vinegar. Pour the dry ingredients into the wet and mix until well combined. Fold in the blueberries, and then pour the mixture into the prepared loaf pan. Bake for 40 to 50 minutes, or until a toothpick inserted in the middle of the loaf comes out clean. Allow to cool for 20 minutes before slicing.

YIELD: 8 servings

BLUEBERRY MUFFINS

Made with quick-burning fuel from the coconut oil, brain-boosting eggs, and antioxidant-rich blueberries (which are linked to improvements in learning, thinking, and memory), these delicious muffins were made with mental focus in mind. These are one of our favorite snacks to eat during the week. On Sundays I make a double batch and freeze them for the week. The night before, I'll place a couple in the fridge so they are ready to be packed for school/work the next day.

½ cup (56 g) coconut flour

⅓ cup (64 g) coconut palm sugar

½ teaspoon baking soda

½ teaspoon sea salt

6 eggs, at room temperature

1 tablespoon (15 ml) vanilla extract

1 teaspoon maple syrup (optional)

⅓ cup (72 g) coconut oil, melted

1 cup (145 g) organic blueberries (fresh or frozen and thawed)

Preheat the oven to 350°F (180°C, or gas mark 4). Line a 12-cup muffin pan with silicone or paper muffin liners, or grease the cups.

In a small bowl, mix together the coconut flour, coconut palm sugar, baking soda, and salt. In a medium bowl, whisk together the eggs, vanilla, and maple syrup (if using). Add the egg mixture to the flour mixture and stir, or use a handheld mixer to combine until smooth. Pour the coconut oil into the bowl and blend well. Fold in the blueberries.

Pour the batter into the prepared muffin cups about two-thirds full. Bake for 20 minutes, or until a toothpick inserted into the middle of a muffin comes out clean.

YIELD: 12 muffins

AT-HOME SNACKS

Use Your Home-Field Advantage for the Tastiest and Healthiest Snack Options

It is four in the afternoon. Dinner isn't for another couple of hours. You're hungry. Your kids, if you have them, are tugging at your pant leg begging for food as if they've never been fed. You step to the pantry and stare into an unsatisfying abyss of prepackaged saltiness.

If you are like most Americans, you tear open a bag of chips or throw some popcorn at the problem. The moment that bag rips open, you've lost. The endorphin rush of the first bite will lead to the second, then the third, and before you know it, there is no room left for a healthy dinner, leading to the inevitable eat-your-vegetables debate. Worse, the nutritional merit of that snack-cum-dinner was abysmal.

If any of the above sounds familiar, this chapter will change your world.

There is a much more healthy, tasty, and satisfying approach to at-home snacks, and the recipes in this chapter are aimed at turning this traditionally nutritional void into something much more beneficial. All that is needed is a little (less than 10 minutes) of prep time and, potentially, a little marketing skill and resolve.

1) Preparation If you are making and serving snacks at home, you have the advantage of an oven. Use that advantage to serve aromatic, warm snacks, which, I promise, are more appetizing than something pulled from a box or bag. Conversely, on a warm summer day, retrieving a cool treat from the fridge will get everyone excited about snack time.

2) Marketing Say this aloud: "It isn't a snack, it's an appetizer." That statement has benefited the eating habits of so many of my clients, typically using vegetable recipes in this chapter. After all, who doesn't love appetizers?

That's what fancy people eat at restaurants. Appetizers at home? What a delight. And, likely, your family will eat more kale chips (or whatever veggie) than if you had set them on their plates at dinnertime. This one is win-win.

3) Resolve Whether it is your family or yourself, change can be a struggle. If the norm is chips and you prepare something new, don't relent. Let the new snack be the only snack. If they are hungry enough, then they will eat it; and if they don't, well then, they really weren't that hungry.

A more likely test of your resolve will concern whether these healthy snacks, which are being aggressively devoured, are going to ruin everyone's appetite for dinner. We usually have our "appetizers" around 4:30 or even 5 p.m.—just when tummies start grumbling but still an hour or two before dinner. With the veggie "appetizers," you don't have to worry about anyone getting overly stuffed. Unlike traditional processed snacks, whole-food "appetizers" appropriately trigger satiation receptors in the brain, so no one will overeat. But worst case, if they do, they will have filled up on nutritious vegetables. I'd say that is also win-win.

  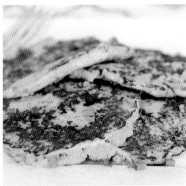

CRISPY OKRA STICKS

These are my go-to whenever I'm in the mood for something crispy and salty. Eat them while they are fresh out of the oven and they will make traditional potato chips seem boring and bland. They really satisfy a salt tooth while simultaneously filling you with a nutrient-dense, fiber-rich, and bone-strengthening veggie.

½ pound (225 g) fresh okra

1 to 2 tablespoons (13.5 to 27 g) coconut oil, melted

¼ teaspoon sea salt

Preheat the oven to 425°F (220°C, or gas mark 7). Rinse and dry the okra, then slice each pod in half lengthwise. Place in a mixing bowl and coat in melted coconut oil and salt. Lay the okra flat on a baking sheet (without parchment paper) and bake for 10 minutes. Turn the okra and bake for another 10 minutes, or until crispy. Serve immediately.

YIELD: about 4 servings

GREEN DEVILED EGGS & BACON

One of my favorite things to have for breakfast is scrambled eggs with avocado and a side of bacon. These are a great way to have that yummy, healthy breakfast as a fun, handheld snack.

4 slices nitrite-free bacon

4 eggs

1 ripe avocado

2 teaspoons (10 ml) hot sauce

Juice from ¼ lime

¼ teaspoon sea salt

Dash of garlic powder

Dash of smoked paprika, for topping (optional)

Preheat the oven to 375°F (190°C, or gas mark 5). Line a baking sheet with aluminum foil. Set the bacon on a baking rack, if you have one, on the baking sheet and bake for 10 minutes on each side.

Meanwhile, place the eggs in a saucepan and cover them by 1 to 2 inches (2.5 to 5 cm) of cold water. (Starting with cold water will help keep them from cracking.) Bring the water to a boil over high heat, then remove the pan from the heat, cover, and let sit for 12 minutes. Pour out the hot water and replace with cold.

While your eggs and bacon are cooking, in a small bowl, combine the avocado, hot sauce, lime juice, salt, and garlic powder. Mix until fairly smooth.

When the eggs are cold, peel them and cut in half lengthwise. Gently remove the yolk and discard. Rinse the egg white if necessary, and place facedown on a paper towel to dry. Spoon the avocado mixture into the yolk hole. If you want to make it look pretty, cut about ¼ inch (6 mm) from the bottom corner of a sandwich bag, put the avocado mixture in, and squeeze it into the eggs.

Once the bacon has cooled and you have patted off the grease, crumble the bacon into bits and add to the top of the avocado-filled eggs. Sprinkle paprika on top, if desired.

YIELD: 4 servings

KALE SALAD

Who knew kale could make such a delightfully mild and tasty salad? Because kale leaves don't get soggy and they soak in flavor over time, this is a great recipe to make and store in your fridge for a delicious superfood snack any time. To make this salad nut-free, either omit the almonds or substitute roasted pepitas.

For salad:

- 1 bunch Tuscan kale
- 1½ cups (132 g) brussels sprouts, grated or finely sliced (optional)
- 3 tablespoons (21 g) sliced almonds
- 3 tablespoons (23 g) dried cranberries
- ½ cup (50 g) grated Parmesan cheese, (optional)

For dressing:

- ½ cup (120 ml) extra-virgin olive oil
- 3 tablespoons (45 ml) fresh lemon juice
- 1½ tablespoons (23 g) Dijon mustard
- 1 shallot, minced
- 2 small cloves garlic, minced
- 1 teaspoon sea salt
- Freshly ground black pepper

To make the salad: Remove the stems from the kale and roughly chop the leaves. You should have about 4 cups (220 g). Place in a large mixing bowl. Add the brussels sprouts, if using, along with the almonds, cranberries, and Parmesan.

To make the dressing: In a small bowl, mix together the olive oil, lemon juice, mustard, shallot, garlic, salt, and pepper. Pour the dressing over the kale mixture, and toss well. Let marinate in the fridge for at least 1 hour.

The salad lasts, covered, for about 3 days in the fridge.

YIELD: 4 servings

CAULIFLOWER HUMMUS

Light and fluffy, this snack tastes even better than traditional hummus. It has all the wonderful flavors of a fabulous Greek snack, but without the difficult-to-digest legumes.

1 medium head cauliflower (about 2 cups [200 g] florets)

⅓ cup (80 g) tahini

¼ cup (60 ml) fresh lemon juice

2 tablespoons (28 ml) extra-virgin olive oil

1 clove garlic

¾ teaspoon sea salt

Black pepper, to taste

Dash of smoked paprika (optional)

Place a steamer basket in a medium pot and fill the pot with about 2 inches (5 cm) of water. If you don't have a basket, use a colander on top of your pot. Bring the water to a boil. Place the cauliflower florets in the steamer basket or colander. Cover and allow the cauliflower to steam for 8 minutes, or until soft. Transfer the cauliflower to a food processor. Add the tahini, lemon juice, olive oil, garlic, salt, and pepper. Blend until smooth. That's it! Dust with smoked paprika, if desired, before serving.

This hummus goes great with My Favorite Crunchy Crackers (page 114) or with any sliced raw veggies.

YIELD: 4 to 6 servings

TIP: Serve the hummus while it's warm and you can be sure it will be devoured quickly.

EASY "CHEESY" KALE CHIPS

Kale chips can be a little tricky to make. The key is to tinker with your oven temperature until you can attain the right level of kale crispiness. But once you get it, you will see just how easy and well worth it it is to make this family staple snack of ours. We (the four of us) can go through two pans' worth of kale in a matter of minutes! Nutritional yeast is the perfect, nutrient-dense, and vitamin B–filled ingredient to make these chips have that yummy cheesy taste. And no one will know it's superhealthy—or dairy-free!

1 bunch kale

2 tablespoons (27 g) coconut oil, melted

¼ cup (28 g) cashew flour or crushed cashews

¼ cup (25 g) nutritional yeast

½ teaspoon sea salt

Preheat the oven to 300°F (150°C, or gas mark 2). Line a baking sheet with parchment paper.

Wash the kale and dry with paper towels. Cut the spine off each piece of kale and then cut the leaves in half. (I don't chop it into small pieces, but you may certainly do so.) Place the leaves in a bowl with the coconut oil, and toss until the leaves are well coated. Set each piece of kale on the prepared baking sheet.

In a small bowl, mix together the cashew flour, nutritional yeast, and salt, and then sprinkle it over the kale to coat. Bake for 25 minutes.

Turn off the heat and let the chips sit in the oven, with the door closed, for at least 30 minutes, until crisp. You might have to play with your oven to get just the right temp/time because everyone's oven is different.

Many times I'll bake them in the morning and let them sit in the oven for a couple of hours. By lunchtime, we will have optimally crunchy, warm kale chips waiting in the oven.

YIELD: about 8 servings (or 4 if you're my family!)

CREAMY ZUCCHINI

With a buttery, creamy, and smooth texture, this treat will change the way you think about zucchini. What's more, this recipe is very simple to prepare and can serve as a great appetizer.

2 or 3 medium zucchini

¼ teaspoon sea salt

1 tablespoon (14 g) ghee or grass-fed butter

1 ripe avocado

Juice from ½ lemon

10 cherry tomatoes, halved

Handful of fresh basil, chopped

Peel the zucchini, and then grate it into fine strands. Set aside on paper towels to absorb some of the excess moisture and sprinkle with salt. The zucchini will start to "sweat" from the salt. Let it sit for about 30 minutes, then use paper towels or a dish towel to squeeze out the excess water.

In a large skillet over medium-high heat, add the ghee and sauté the zucchini, stirring every couple of minutes, until the zucchini starts to brown. It may take longer than you think (15 or so minutes), especially if you didn't squeeze enough moisture out. Once brown, remove from the heat and set aside.

Mash the avocado in a medium bowl until creamy. Add the lemon juice, tomatoes, and basil, and stir until combined. Mix in the warm zucchini, stir to combine, and serve immediately.

YIELD: 2 to 4 servings

BUTTERNUT SQUASH FRITTERS

These distinctive flat cakes are flavorful and fun to eat. You could eat them alone with your hands or add some cheese (if you eat dairy) to make grilled cheese sandwiches. While these are a favorite of mine, what I love even more about them is that they are a superhealthy snack loaded with vitamin A, a known bone builder and heart protector, as well as vitamin C, which will help keep colds at bay. To save on prep time, buy 12 ounces (340 g) precut squash in the refrigerator or freezer section.

1 small butternut squash, peeled, seeded, and roughly chopped (about 3 cups, or 340 g)

2 eggs

1 tablespoon (7 g) coconut flour

1 tablespoon (6 g) sliced scallions

1 tablespoon (7 g) onion powder

1 teaspoon ground sage

1 teaspoon dried cilantro or 1 tablespoon [1 g] fresh chopped

1 teaspoon sea salt

1 teaspoon gluten-free hot sauce (such as Texas Pete's)

½ teaspoon garlic powder

¼ teaspoon black pepper

1 tablespoon ghee, grass-fed butter, or coconut oil, for frying

Set a steamer basket in a medium pot and fill the pot with about 2 inches (5 cm) of water. If you don't have a basket, use a colander on top of your pot. Bring the water to a boil. Place the butternut squash pieces in the steamer basket or colander. Cover and allow the squash to steam for 7 minutes, or until fork-tender. Then, mash it in a mixing bowl until it is puréed. Add the eggs, coconut flour, scallions, onion powder, sage, cilantro, salt, hot sauce, garlic powder, and pepper and combine well. Shape into patties about 2 inches (5 cm) in diameter.

In a large skillet over medium-high heat, melt the ghee. Place as many patties into the skillet as you can without them touching. Cook until the edges become light brown. Carefully flip the fritters and allow them to brown on the other side. Reduce the heat to low and cook for 5 or so more minutes, or until cooked through.

YIELD: 6 to 8 cakes

PROSCIUTTO-WRAPPED ASPARAGUS

With just three simple ingredients, this supertasty snack is a great late-afternoon treat. My kids will snatch them off the plate and eat them with their hands like a pretzel stick. Before you know it, they're all gone . . . and, that's a good thing!

1 pound (455 g) fresh asparagus

4 ounces (115 g) thinly sliced prosciutto

1 tablespoon (14 g) ghee or grass-fed butter

Cut the bottom 2 inches (5 cm) off the asparagus. Then cut each slice of prosciutto in half lengthwise and individually wrap each piece around an asparagus spear.

In a large skillet over medium-high heat, melt the ghee. Add the wrapped asparagus and cook for about 2 minutes on each side, until the prosciutto is crispy. Reduce the heat to low and cook for about 10 minutes so the asparagus can steam.

Alternatively, you can roast them at 450°F (230°C, or gas mark 8) on a baking sheet. After you've wrapped the asparagus with prosciutto, brush them with melted ghee/butter, bake for 5 minutes on one side, flip, and let bake for an additional 5 minutes.

YIELD: 4 servings

SQUASH CHIPS

Crunchy, salty squash chips have always been a family favorite. In addition to being high in antioxidants and vitamin C, squash is a good source of manganese, a mineral that helps the body process fats, carbohydrates, and glucose. This chip will squash any traditional packaged "chip" out there.

3 medium yellow squash or zucchini

Coconut oil spray or regular coconut oil

Dash of sea salt

Dash of garlic powder

Dash of Parmesan cheese (optional)

Preheat the oven to 450°F (230°C, or gas mark 8). Grease or spray a baking sheet with coconut oil.

Slice the squash into thin chips of a consistent thickness. A mandolin slicer will help greatly here.

Lay the squash flat on the baking sheet. Coat the squash chips with oil. Sprinkle the salt, garlic powder, and cheese, if desired.

Bake for about 10 minutes, or until they start to brown, and then turn the chips. Bake for an additional 5 minutes, or until they start to brown. Turn off the heat and let the chips sit in the oven for an hour.

Be sure to check on them periodically so they don't burn. Letting them sit will help them crisp up, but if you don't have time to wait, just bake them an additional 5 to 7 minutes until they are brown.

YIELD: 4 servings

ONION RINGS

Do you ever miss fried foods? You won't need to after eating these. This healthy take on onion rings is packed with protein and fiber from the almond meal and healthy fats from the shredded coconut and coconut oil. I don't think many restaurants can make that same claim. (Can you say gluten and hydrogenated oils?)

2 cups (160 g) unsweetened shredded coconut

1½ cups (150 g) almond meal

¼ cup (32 g) arrowroot powder

1 tablespoon (9 g) garlic powder

1 tablespoon (7 g) smoked paprika

2 teaspoons (5 g) onion powder

2 teaspoons (12 g) sea salt

1 teaspoon black pepper

2 eggs

½ teaspoon apple cider vinegar

1 tablespoon (15 ml) unsweetened canned coconut milk (stirred first) or almond milk

2 medium onions

3 to 4 tablespoons (40 to 54 g) coconut oil, for frying

In a quart-size (1 L) resealable freezer bag, mix together the coconut, almond meal, arrowroot, garlic powder, paprika, onion powder, salt, and pepper. In a small bowl, whisk together the eggs, vinegar, and milk and set aside.

Slice the onions to desired ring thickness and separate the rings. Dip them in the egg mixture, then put them in the bag with the dry ingredients and shake until evenly coated.

In a large skillet over medium-high heat, heat the coconut oil. Carefully place the onion rings into the skillet and fry for about 3 minutes on each side, or until brown. When they are done, place them on a paper towel–lined plate or a metal rack to cool. Enjoy while warm!

Alternatively, you can bake the onion rings on the top rack of a 425°F (220°C, or gas mark 7) oven for 15 to 20 minutes, or until brown.

YIELD: 4 servings

ZESTY WALNUT BRUSSELS SPROUTS

These brussels sprouts will please just about anyone's taste buds, thanks to a zing from the lemon juice. Be sure to make enough for leftovers, because they soak in flavor over time and are even better the next day.

½ cup (60 g) walnuts, chopped

1 pound (455 g) brussels sprouts, halved or quartered

2 to 3 tablespoons (27 to 40 g) coconut oil, melted

½ teaspoon sea salt

Black pepper, to taste

2 tablespoons (28 ml) extra-virgin olive oil

Juice from ½ lemon

Preheat the oven to 350°F (180°C, or gas mark 4). Scatter the walnuts on a baking sheet and bake for 10 minutes, or until toasted and fragrant. Set aside to cool.

Increase the oven to 400°F (200°C, or gas mark 6). Line a baking sheet with parchment paper.

In a medium bowl, toss together the brussels sprouts, coconut oil, salt, and pepper. Lay the sprouts out on the prepared baking sheet and roast for 35 minutes, or until fork-tender. (I recommend stirring them halfway through baking to help cook evenly.)

Place the sprouts in a bowl, and mix in the walnuts, olive oil, and lemon juice.

Store any leftovers in the fridge and then eat cool, or warm briefly in the microwave or a pan.

YIELD: 4 to 6 servings

SWEET BACON KALE

This easy-to-make and supertasty snack is sweet, salty, and so good you'll forget you're eating a superfood.

3	slices nitrate-free bacon, chopped into bite-size pieces
4	big handfuls kale, torn from stems
1	tablespoon (15 ml) apple cider vinegar
¼	teaspoon sea salt
2 or 3	drops liquid stevia

In a large skillet over medium heat, cook the bacon until brown and crispy, 8 to 10 minutes. Add the kale and cook for 5 minutes, or until the leaves soften. Mix in the apple cider vinegar, salt, and stevia. Serve immediately or save in the fridge for a snack later on.

YIELD: about 4 servings

SOFT PALEO PRETZELS

Who doesn't love pretzels? Not only are they fun to eat, but these are fun to make as well. And without the gluten found in most pretzels or the superhigh glycemic load of gluten-free pretzels, you can feel good about eating this snack. What is particularly great about these is you can give them a touch of

3 eggs, at room temperature, divided

2 tablespoons (28 g) grass-fed butter, melted, divided

1½ cups (168 g) almond flour

3 tablespoons (21 g) coconut flour, divided

2 tablespoons (16 g) psyllium husk powder

½ teaspoon fine sea salt

1 teaspoon water

Coarse sea salt, to taste

In a small bowl, whisk together 2 of the eggs and 1 tablespoon (14 g) of the butter. In a medium bowl, mix together the almond flour, 1 tablespoon (7 g) of the coconut flour, psyllium husk powder, and fine sea salt. (If desired, stir in alternative flavorings at this point.) Then add in the eggs-butter mixture until well combined. Let sit for a few minutes, as it takes some time for the coconut flour to be absorbed. Add a second tablespoon (7 g) of coconut flour, and stir well. Stir in the last tablespoon (7 g) of coconut flour. The goal is to produce a dough that can be easily kneaded, without sticking to your hands.

Allow the dough to rest for 5 minutes. Preheat the oven to 350°F (180°C, or gas mark 4). Line a baking sheet with parchment paper.

Place a hunk of dough about the size of a golf ball on the sheet. Roll the dough under your hands and make it as thin or thick as you would like. We make ours pencil thin, but feel free to get creative and make any shape or size pretzel you would like. Repeat with the remaining dough and then bake for about 10 minutes. If yours are thicker, they may need to bake a bit longer. You'll know they're done when a toothpick inserted in the middle of the thickest part of the pretzel comes out clean.

While the pretzels are in the oven, beat together the remaining egg with the water.

Remove the pretzels from the oven and increase the oven temperature to 400°F (200°C, or gas mark 6). Turn all of the pretzels over and you will see the bottom is nicely browned. Lightly brush

sweetness by adding 1 teaspoon cinnamon and 2 teaspoons (8 g) coconut palm sugar. Alternatively, you can morph them into Italian breadsticks through a dash of garlic and onion powder (1 teaspoon each). They're very versatile!

the browned part of the pretzels with the egg mixture and sprinkle with the coarse salt. Return to the oven for 5 minutes. Brush the remaining 1 tablespoon (14 g) of butter on top of the pretzels when pulled from the oven.

If desired, sprinkle cinnamon and/or coconut palm sugar on top.

YIELD: 6 to 8 pretzels

RANCH "CHEESE" BALL

Cheese balls are so tasty, and they go well with crackers—especially My Favorite Crunchy Crackers (page 114). While this cheese ball is missing the dairy, it is certainly not missing any flavor!

For ball:

- 2 cups (290 g) raw or dry-roasted (unsalted) cashews, macadamia nuts, and/or Marcona almonds (or a mix of any nut you choose without skins)
- 3 tablespoons (45 ml) extra-virgin olive oil
- 2 tablespoons (28 ml) water
- Juice of ½ lemon (about 2 tablespoons, or 28 ml)
- ¼ cup (12 g) thinly sliced chives
- ¼ cup (15 g) Italian parsley, chopped
- 2 cloves garlic, minced
- 1 teaspoon onion powder
- 1 teaspoon sea salt

For topping:

- ¼ cup (32 g) sesame seeds
- ¼ cup (20 g) bacon bits
- 2 tablespoons (4 g) dried onion
- 2 tablespoons (16 g) poppy seeds
- 1 tablespoon (6 g) ground black pepper

To make the ball: In a food processor, process the nuts until well chopped. In a small bowl, mix together the olive oil, water, and lemon juice. Slowly pour the liquid mixture into the food processor with the nuts and blend until smooth and creamy. Place the nut mixture in a bowl and add the chives, parsley, garlic, onion powder, and salt, tasting to check for desired seasoning.

To make the topping: In a pie plate or medium bowl, mix together the sesame seeds, bacon bits, dried onion, poppy seeds, and pepper. With your hands, roll the mixture into a large ball. Roll the ball onto the toppings and press firmly and evenly. Refrigerate for at least an hour before serving to let it firm up and allow the flavors to meld. Serve with raw vegetables or crackers.

YIELD: about 8 servings

ROASTED RED PEPPER DIP

We all know how vitamin C is great for the common cold, but did you also know that it helps protect us from the harmful effects of stress? Vitamin C allows the body to quickly clear out cortisol, a primary stress hormone that increases sugars in the bloodstream. And, it just so happens that red peppers are the second highest plant source of vitamin C, containing almost 300 percent of our daily vitamin C intake. Mix all of that into a divine-tasting dip and you've got a superb snack!

1 cup (100 g) shelled walnuts

1 teaspoon smoked paprika

½ teaspoon onion powder

½ teaspoon sea salt

1 jar (12 ounces, or 340 g) roasted red peppers, drained

1 clove garlic, minced

2 tablespoons (28 ml) extra-virgin olive oil

2 teaspoons (10 ml) lemon juice

In a food processor, pulse the walnuts, paprika, onion powder, and salt until the walnuts are finely ground (like the consistency of hummus). Add the peppers, garlic, olive oil, and lemon juice and blend until completely smooth.

YIELD: about 4 servings

ARTICHOKE PESTO

Pesto is a fabulous snack because it is so full of flavor; it can make anything taste great. And, thanks to the anti-inflammatory olive oil, the high amount of fiber from the artichokes, the detoxifying properties of the basil and garlic, and the omega-3s from the walnuts, this snack not only tastes amazing, but it also acts as a nutritional powerhouse for the body.

1	cup (100 g) walnuts
1	cup (235 ml) extra-virgin olive oil
8 to 10	cloves garlic
1	can (14 ounces, or 400 g) or ½ cup (150 g) quartered artichoke hearts in water, drained
1	tablespoon (15 ml) lemon juice
½	teaspoon sea salt
	Approximately 5½ cups (220 g) fresh basil

In a food processor, process the walnuts, olive oil, garlic, artichoke hearts, lemon juice, salt, and basil until smooth. Taste and adjust for seasoning. Then enjoy on crackers, chicken, eggs, salad, you name it!

YIELD: 2¼ cups (585 g)

TIP: If you sauté your artichoke hearts and garlic cloves in 1 tablespoon of butter or ghee before blending, the flavor will pop even more!

PANCAKE-WRAPPED SAUSAGE

This protein-packed wrapped snack is great for a mid-morning or even late-afternoon snack. It's fun to eat and similar to a corn dog (you could even add a stick or toothpick). With a touch of sweetness, this snack will be loved by all.

10   precooked organic sausage links (such as Applegate Breakfast Sausage), cut in half

1½   cups (168 g) almond flour

¼   cup (20 g) unsweetened shredded coconut

1   tablespoon (8 g) arrowroot powder

¼   teaspoon baking soda

¼   teaspoon sea salt

2   eggs

½   cup (120 ml) unsweetened canned coconut milk (stirred first)

1   tablespoon (20 g) maple syrup

1   teaspoon vanilla extract

1 or 2   tablespoons (13.5 to 27 g) coconut oil or grass-fed butter, for cooking

In a large skillet over low heat, warm up the sausage links and then set them aside.

In a medium bowl, mix together the almond flour, coconut, arrowroot, baking soda, and salt. In a small bowl, whisk together the eggs, coconut milk, maple syrup, and vanilla. Stir the coconut milk mixture into the dry ingredients and blend until smooth.

Return the large skillet to medium heat, and add 1 tablespoon (13.5 g) of the coconut oil. Slowly pour the pancake mix in the shape of small rectangles as best you can. Lay half a sausage link in the middle of each rectangle and pour a little more batter to cover the link. Cook until the pancake bottom browns, about 3 minutes. Carefully flip and cook for a few more minutes, until the other side browns. Repeat with the reamining batter and sausages, adding more oil as needed.

YIELD: 20 snacks

GREEN LEMONADE SMOOTHIE

While smoothies can be healthy, too often they are overloaded with high-sugar fruits, which, while fine in moderation, can spike insulin levels when overused. This carefully formulated smoothie tastes great, doesn't contain too much sugar, and balances an appropriate amount of protein, fat, and fiber. As a bonus, it is brimming with vitamins and minerals our bodies need.

¾ cup (175 ml) coconut water

¼ cup (60 ml) almond milk

2 or 3 handfuls spinach

2 or 3 handfuls kale (stems removed)

1 tablespoon (11 g) flaxseeds

Juice of 1 lemon or lime (about 3 tablespoons, or 45 ml)

A big scoop of ice (about 1 cup, or 140 g)

1 medium green apple, cored

1 banana

To a blender, add the coconut water, almond milk, spinach, kale, flaxseeds, and lemon juice. Blend on high until smooth. Toss in the ice, apple, and banana, and blend until the desired consistency.

YIELD: 1 or 2 servings

EASY-BAKE CAKE CUP

When I am having a sweet tooth or craving something carby, this little snack hits the spot. While it satisfies a craving, it also fills you up with fiber and protein. The individual size is ideal for this afternoon treat.

1 egg

2 tablespoons (14 g) almond flour

1 tablespoon (7 g) coconut flour

1 tablespoon (12 g) coconut palm sugar

1 tablespoon (11 g) dark chocolate chips

1 tablespoon (5 g) raw cacao powder (optional)

Pinch of baking soda

Dash of sea salt

In a microwave-safe cup, mix together the egg, almond flour, coconut flour, coconut palm sugar, dark chocolate chips, cacao powder (if using), baking soda, and salt. Microwave on high for 90 seconds. Simple as that!

YIELD: 1 serving

ENERGIZING CHOCOLATE MILK OR HOT CHOCOLATE

A few years ago, I quit drinking coffee—a twenty-five-year habit. Some days, I find I still want a pick-me-up, and this drink can satisfy a coffee craving along with giving me a little energy boost. The good news is that a cup of this is loaded with more antioxidants than blueberries or green tea; it has more iron than spinach, and a big serving of magnesium to boot. Take that, coffee!

2 tablespoons (28 ml) water

1 to 2 tablespoons (12 to 24 g) coconut palm sugar

1 tablespoon (5 g) raw cacao powder

1 cup (235 ml) almond milk

In a microwave-safe mug, heat the water in the microwave on high for 30 seconds. Mix in the coconut palm sugar and cacao powder so it turns into a thin pastelike consistency. Stir in the almond milk and enjoy!

If you wish to make hot chocolate instead, use canned full-fat coconut milk instead of almond milk to get a creamier texture. Just heat all of the ingredients together in a small saucepan over medium-low heat and add a little vanilla extract (¼ to ½ teaspoon).

YIELD: 1 serving

ON-THE-GO SNACKS

Fun and Convenient Treats for Road Trips, Commutes, and Carpools

We spend a great deal of our lives in the car. It's a necessary part of life, particularly if you live in a suburban area. And whether you are going to work, driving a carpool to a child's activity, or even heading out on a fun road trip, choosing the right snacks can be daunting. What can you bring that is portable, tasty, easy to eat, fun (especially if it's for a road trip), keeps well, and of course, is actually good for you?

If you've ever tried to reach a destination with screaming, fighting, or fussy children in the backseat (or a cranky spouse in the passenger seat), you probably learned that they don't complain as much when they're munching on something yummy. After all, fussiness is often a signal for hunger in smaller children (and even some adults). The problem is that many prepackaged snacks are laden with preservatives and food coloring that, according to recent research by the UK's government-sponsored Food Commission, could actually increase temper tantrums and irritable behavior.

And what about all that sugar found in most prepackaged snacks? According to Sally Fallon, a researcher at the Weston A. Price Foundation, research shows that "destructive, aggressive and restless behavior is significantly correlated with the amount of sugar" we eat or drink. Keep that in mind the next time you plan to hop into the car for a long road trip with a bag full of sugary snacks. It just might be you who's asking, "Are we there yet?"

Fortunately for you, this chapter contains many delicious snacks that are both fun and easy to eat—no spoon feeding or face wiping of little ones. They're made with no artificial colors, additives, or processed sugar. Even better, because they're low-glycemic, they will keep blood sugar levels stable to avoid any hyperactive highs or grouchy lows.

Moreover, all these snacks fit neatly into sandwich bags and/or small storage containers, making it nice and easy for you to turn to the back-seat at a stoplight and pass out treats everyone will enjoy, keeping them happy for both the short term, and, literally, down the road.

CINNAMON GRAHAM CRACKERS

This delicious cracker reminds me of the classic snack I grew up eating. While these crackers are a real treat when combined with a nut butter, they are also great alone. And they're pretty simple to make, which is a good thing because they get gobbled up quickly!

2 cups (224 g) almond flour

1 cup (128 g) arrowroot powder

6 tablespoons (120 g) maple syrup

1 tablespoon (7 g) cinnamon

½ teaspoon sea salt

Additional cinnamon and coconut palm sugar, for dusting

Preheat the oven to 350°F (180°C, or gas mark 4). Put the almond flour, arrowroot powder, maple syrup, cinnamon, and salt into a food processor and process until the mixture thickens and becomes doughy.

Place the dough on a sheet of parchment paper. Using another large piece of parchment paper on top of the mixture, press or roll the dough with a rolling pin until it becomes flat and thin (about ¼ inch, or 6 mm).

Remove the top piece of parchment. With a pizza cutter, cut the dough into 2½ x 2½-inch (6.5 x 6.5 cm) squares (or rectangles or whatever shape you prefer). For the classic graham cracker look, poke holes with a toothpick. Transfer the dough on the bottom piece of parchment to a baking sheet.

Bake for 6 to 8 minutes, or until set. Then dust with coconut palm sugar and cinnamon. Place on a cooling rack for about 45 minutes and then enjoy a trip back to childhood.

YIELD: about 14 crackers

CHOCOLATE ALMOND SQUARES

This snack is one of my favorites, probably because it tastes like a dessert. With healthy coconut meat, coconut oil, almonds, and low-glycemic sugars, this snack can be enjoyed guilt-free! If you are watching your sugar intake, feel free to use less dark chocolate or a chocolate with a higher percentage of cacao. I typically use 70 percent cacao dark chocolate.

1¼ cups (138 g) sliced almonds

1 cup (80 g) unsweetened shredded coconut

⅓ cup (58 g) dark chocolate chips

2 tablespoons (24 g) coconut palm sugar

¼ teaspoon salt

¼ cup (85 g) coconut nectar

2 tablespoons (27 g) coconut oil

1½ teaspoons (7.5 ml) vanilla extract

Dash of coarse sea salt, for topping

Preheat the oven to 300°F (150°C, or gas mark 2). Grease an 8 × 8-inch (20 × 20 cm) baking dish.

In a food processor, pulse the almonds for a few seconds, just enough to break them up but not enough to become like flour. In a medium bowl, mix together the almonds, coconut, chocolate chips, coconut palm sugar, and salt. In a small saucepan over medium-low heat, cook the coconut nectar, coconut oil, and vanilla for about 5 minutes, or until it starts to bubble. Pour the warm liquid into the dry mixture and stir until everything is well coated.

Pour the mixture into the prepared baking dish. With your hands or a piece of parchment paper, firmly press to make sure the mixture is flat and even. Sprinkle some coarse salt on top, and bake for 30 minutes, or until the bars feel firm to the touch. Allow to cool for 2 to 3 hours or put in the fridge for an hour so it can set. Cut into bars and store in the fridge.

YIELD: 12 bars

CHOCOLATE CHIP GRANOLA SQUARES

With powerful omega-3 fats to help lower your blood pressure and risk of heart attacks (driving can be stressful!) and lots of fiber and good fat to keep you full, this wonderful-tasting snack is great for on the road, and it's loved by all!

½ cup (73 g) raw almonds

½ cup (73 g) raw cashews

1 cup (80 g) unsweetened shredded coconut

¼ cup (41 g) chia seeds

2 tablespoons (22 g) flaxseeds

¼ cup (44 g) dark chocolate chips, plus a handful for topping

¼ teaspoon fine sea salt

½ cup (170 g) dark raw honey

2 tablespoons (27 g) coconut oil

¼ teaspoon vanilla extract

Dash of coarse sea salt, for topping

Preheat the oven to 350°F (180°C, or gas mark 4). Grease an 8 × 8-inch (20 × 20 cm) baking dish.

In a food processor, lightly chop the almonds and cashews. Transfer to a medium bowl, then stir in the coconut, chia seeds, flaxseeds, ¼ cup (44 g) of the chocolate chips, and fine salt.

In a small saucepan over medium-low heat, cook the honey, coconut oil, and vanilla until it starts to bubble, 3 to 4 minutes. Pour the liquid mixture into the bowl of nuts and seeds, and stir it all together. (The chocolate will melt with the hot mixture, but that's okay because you'll put some chocolate chips on top at the end.)

Place the mixture in the baking dish. Take a piece of parchment paper and place it on top of the granola. Press down firmly, so you can even it out and make sure it's packed in there tightly. Sprinkle coarse salt and the remaining handful of chocolate chips on top. Bake for 16 minutes, or until firm to the touch. Allow it to cool for a few hours (you can put it in the fridge) before cutting into squares. Store in the fridge.

YIELD: 12 to 15 bars

PUMPKIN BARS

My kids literally jump up and down with excitement for these bars. These savory treats are perfectly sweetened. With a whole cup of pumpkin in the mix, this snack is full of fiber to keep you full, as well as vitamin A and iron to help keep immune systems strong.

1 cup (245 g) pumpkin purée

½ cup (130 g) smooth almond butter

⅓ cup (64 g) coconut palm sugar

1 tablespoon (7 g) coconut flour

1 tablespoon (7 g) pumpkin pie spice

1 tablespoon (20 g) maple syrup

½ teaspoon vanilla extract

2 eggs

¼ teaspoon baking soda

⅛ teaspoon sea salt

Handful of walnuts, chopped (optional)

Preheat the oven to 350°F (180°C, or gas mark 4). Grease an 8 × 8-inch (20 × 20 cm) baking dish.

In a large bowl (or food processor), mix together the pumpkin purée, almond butter, palm sugar, coconut flour, pumpkin pie spice, maple syrup, vanilla, eggs, baking soda, and salt until well blended. Pour the mixture into the prepared baking dish. Bake for about 40 minutes, or until a toothpick inserted in the middle comes out clean. Allow to cool for about 30 minutes and then eat as is or top with chopped walnuts.

YIELD: 12 bars

ALMOND CHEESE CRACKERS

Reminiscent of a popular childhood snack but way better for you, these crispy crackers are really tasty, especially with Cauliflower Hummus (page 75). With loads of different B vitamins from the nutritional yeast, this cracker can give you a boost of energy!

1¼ cups (140 g) almond flour

¼ cup (32 g) arrowroot powder

¼ cup (25 g) nutritional yeast (or shredded sharp cheese if you do dairy)

1 teaspoon sea salt

½ teaspoon garlic powder

¼ teaspoon onion powder

1 egg

2 tablespoons (28 ml) lemon juice

1 tablespoon (14 g) grass-fed butter or ghee, melted (omit if allergic)

Preheat the oven to 350°F (180°C, or gas mark 4).

In a medium bowl, combine the almond flour, arrowroot powder, nutritional yeast, salt, garlic powder, and onion powder. Once mixed well, add in the egg, lemon juice, and butter and stir until a dough forms.

Place the dough on a piece of parchment paper. Set another piece of parchment paper on top and roll with a rolling pin to about ⅛ inch (3 mm) thick. Remove the top piece of parchment. With a pizza cutter, score your individual crackers into 1-inch (2.5 cm) squares. Use a toothpick to poke one or two holes in the center of each cracker. Transfer the dough and bottom piece of parchment to a baking sheet. Bake for 8 minutes, or until they start to brown and harden. Pull from the oven and allow to cool for about 30 minutes, then break apart into squares

YIELD: about 48 crackers

BUTTERED SALTINE CRACKERS

When I was a little girl, in the wintertime I used to put butter on saltine crackers and then prop them up on a log close to the fire in the fireplace. I'll never forget that warm, buttery, and salty taste. Here's the next best thing, but a heck of a lot better for you.

¾ cup (84 g) almond flour

¼ cup (32 g) arrowroot powder

¼ cup (28 g) coconut flour

½ teaspoon fine sea salt

2 tablespoons (28 g) plus 1 teaspoon grass-fed butter, melted, divided

2 egg whites

½ teaspoon coarse sea salt, for topping

Preheat the oven to 350°F (180°C, or gas mark 4).

Combine the almond flour, arrowroot powder, coconut flour, and fine salt. Once mixed well, add in 2 tablespoons (28 g) of the butter and the egg whites and stir until a dough forms.

Place the dough on a piece of parchment paper. Lay another piece of parchment paper on top and roll with a rolling pin to make it flat, ⅛- to ¼-inch (3 to 6 mm) thick. Remove the top piece of parchment. With a pizza cutter, score into 2-inch (5 cm) square crackers and then use a toothpick to make soda cracker–like holes. Transfer the dough and bottom piece of parchment to a baking sheet.

Bake for 5 minutes, and then brush the remaining 1 teaspoon butter on top of the crackers and sprinkle with the coarse salt. Bake for another 5 minutes, turn the oven off, and allow them to sit for 10 more minutes in the oven. Check on them occasionally, though, to make sure they don't burn, because everyone's oven is different and the thickness of the crackers will vary. Let cool, then break apart into crackers.

YIELD: about 15 crackers

APPLE CRISP CHIPS

Most dried fruits in the grocery store have added sugars and preservatives. It can be difficult to find packaged dried fruit that is organic to boot. These apples are so easy to prepare, and the kids will enjoy helping make this sweet and crunchy snack!

2 apples of choice (we used Pink Lady)

Coconut oil, spray or melted

1 teaspoon cinnamon

1 teaspoon coconut palm sugar

Preheat the oven to 225°F (107°C). Line a baking sheet with parchment paper.

Using a sharp knife or mandolin, slice your apples thinly. They should be about ⅛-inch (3 mm) thick. Take out any seeds you see.

Lay the apple slices flat on the prepared baking sheet and ensure they aren't touching one another. Spray with coconut oil (or melt and brush on) and sprinkle cinnamon and coconut palm sugar over them. Bake for 1 hour and then turn them. Bake for another 1 to 1½ hours, until the apples are crisp. They will get even more crisp as they cool.

YIELD: about 20 chips

SILVER DOLLAR BANANA PANCAKES

These scrumptious little snacks are great for the road because you can eat them alone or with some nut/seed butter. They also freeze well, so they are great for packing on a long trip. Just be sure to take them out of the freezer about three hours before you'll want to eat them. Because they are small, they won't take long to thaw. Just in time for snack time!

2 ripe bananas

3 eggs

3 tablespoons (21 g) coconut flour

1 tablespoon (8 g) arrowroot powder

1 teaspoon vanilla extract

¼ teaspoon baking soda

1 tablespoon (20 g) maple syrup

1 tablespoon (12 g) coconut palm sugar

Sprinkle of cinnamon

Pinch of sea salt

1 tablespoon (14 g) grass-fed butter or coconut oil

In a food processor, combine the bananas, eggs, coconut flour, arrowroot powder, vanilla, baking soda, maple syrup, coconut palm sugar, cinnamon, and salt and blend until smooth.

In a large skillet over medium heat (not any higher because they can scorch easily), melt the butter to coat the skillet. Pour silver dollar–size pancakes. Cook for about 4 minutes, until you see bubbles, and then carefully flip and cook for a couple more minutes, until done.

YIELD: 15 to 18 pancakes

CRISPY MAPLE GRANOLA

This is my favorite granola, bar none. You'll just have to take my word for it and try it. There is something about a salty, sweet, crunchy, and buttery treat all wrapped into one snack that is quite amazing. I also love the health benefits of the grass-fed butter, which include immune-boosting, cancer-fighting, fat-burning nutrients. Also loaded with fiber, omega-3s, and other healthy fats, this snack is great for a car ride as it will keep you satiated a long time, or even at home with some berries and almond or coconut milk.

¾ cup (75 g) raw pecans

½ cup (73 g) raw almonds

½ cup (50 g) raw walnuts

¾ cup (60 g) unsweetened shredded coconut

3 tablespoons (30 g) chia seeds

¼ cup (85 g) maple syrup

2½ tablespoons (35 g) grass-fed butter

1½ teaspoons (7.5 ml) vanilla extract

¼ teaspoon sea salt

Preheat the oven to 325°F (170°C, or gas mark 3). Line a baking sheet with parchment paper.

In a food processor, pulse the pecans, almonds, and walnuts until they are in small pieces. Pour into a medium bowl with the shredded coconut and chia seeds; toss to combine. In a small saucepan over medium-low heat, cook the maple syrup, butter, vanilla, and salt until it starts to bubble. Pour the liquid mixture over the nuts, coconut, and seeds. Mix well.

Spread onto the prepared baking sheet so it's not overlapping too much. Bake for 20 minutes, or until it starts to turn golden brown, tossing a couple of times so it cooks evenly. Once it comes out and starts to cool, it will get crunchier.

YIELD: 3 cups (366 g)

MY FAVORITE CRUNCHY CRACKERS

There is no better name for this cracker. Crackers should be salty, crispy, flavorful, and, well, a little addictive, and this one hits all of those requirements. Fortunately, they are also good for you, as opposed to any traditional or gluten-free crackers from the store. Low-glycemic and full of protein, with good fats including lots of omega-3s, this easy-to-eat snack is ideal for in the car, or anywhere else for that matter.

---

1 cup (112 g) almond flour
½ cup (64 g) flaxseed meal
½ cup (92 g) chia seeds
1¼ teaspoons sea salt
2 teaspoons (3 g) Italian seasoning
1 teaspoon garlic powder
1 egg
2 tablespoons (28 ml) extra-virgin olive oil

Preheat the oven to 350°F (180°C, or gas mark 4).

In a medium bowl, combine the almond flour, flaxseed meal, chia seeds, salt, Italian seasoning, and garlic powder. Once mixed well, add in the egg and olive oil and stir until a dough forms.

Place half of the dough on a piece of parchment paper. Top with another piece of parchment paper and roll with a rolling pin to about ⅛ inch (3 mm) thick. Remove the top piece of parchment. With a pizza cutter, score your individual crackers into squares. Transfer the dough and bottom piece of parchment to a baking sheet. Bake for 8 minutes, or until they start to turn brown. Then turn off the heat and let them sit in the oven for another 10 minutes or so.

Once those are done, you can lay out the second batch on the prepared baking sheet and begin baking them. You can also bake them on two baking sheets, one on each rack in the oven; just shuffle the baking sheets halfway through the baking time. Break apart into crackers once cool.

YIELD: about 50 crackers

FLATCAKE SANDWICH BREAD

This pancake-like bread is delicious with any nut or seed butter. It's fun for the kids to cut out different shapes with a cookie cutter. And, with lots of good fats and protein from the almond flour and fiber from the coconut flour, it will keep them (or you) full for the long haul.

1 cup (112 g) almond flour

¼ cup (28 g) coconut flour

½ teaspoon sea salt

2 eggs

¾ cup (175 ml) unsweetened canned coconut milk (stirred first)

¼ cup (85 g) maple syrup

2 teaspoons (10 ml) vanilla extract

Preheat the oven to 350°F (180°C, or gas mark 4). Line a baking sheet with parchment paper.

Blend together the almond flour, coconut flour, and salt. Add in the eggs, coconut milk, maple syrup, and vanilla and mix with a fork until smooth. Roll the dough out evenly on the prepared baking sheet, and bake for 16 minutes, or until a toothpick inserted in the middle of the bread comes out clean. Let cool for an hour or so before using a cookie cutter, pizza cutter, or knife to cut out your "bread" slices.

YIELD: 6 to 8 "sandwich" slices depending on the cutting method/size

SUPERFRUITY ROLL-UPS

Do most fruit roll-up snacks (or any kind of snack for that matter) have a whole cup of fresh spinach in them and taste amazing? I didn't think so. Because of the vitamins K and A in the spinach, not only does this snack help the body fight off infection and keep the immune system strong, but it also helps support bone growth and healthy eyesight. By using fruits with the lowest amounts of sugar and the highest amount of antioxidants, this snack is a winner all around. You can use fresh or frozen (unsweetened) fruit. If it's frozen, let it thaw before using.

1 cup (145 g) strawberries
1 cup (145 g) wild blueberries
1 cup (30 g) spinach
½ cup (65 g) raspberries
1½ teaspoons (10 g) dark raw honey

Preheat the oven to 200°F (93°C). Line a jelly-roll pan with parchment paper.

Put the strawberries, blueberries, spinach, raspberries, and honey in a high-powered blender (so you can chop up the spinach well) and blend until puréed. Starting in the middle, pour the mixture onto the prepared baking sheet. Use a spatula to even it out as much as you can. You want it to be fairly thin (no more than ¼-inch, or 6 mm, thick) so it can solidify. If it is too thick, it will take longer to congeal. Bake for about 4 hours, or until you can begin to peel it off the paper and it is of fruit roll-up consistency. Cut into 1-inch (2.5 cm) strips or just peel directly off the paper and enjoy!

Stored in an airtight container, the roll-ups should last a couple of weeks. Or you can freeze them for about a year, as long as they're tightly wrapped in plastic wrap.

YIELD: about 15 strips

PINWHEEL SANDWICH BREAD

Whether you cut the "bread" into individual-size pinwheels or eat it as a wrap, this superflavorful seasoned bread makes your avocado, ham, and tomato sandwich healthier and taste better than any sandwich you've ever had.

1 cup (235 ml) unsweetened canned coconut milk (stirred first)

½ cup (56 g) almond flour

½ cup (64 g) arrowroot powder

½ teaspoon garlic powder

½ teaspoon onion powder

¼ teaspoon sea salt

1 tablespoon (14 g) grass-fed butter

In a medium bowl, mix together the coconut milk, almond flour, arrowroot powder, garlic powder, onion powder, and salt until smooth.

Heat a large nonstick skillet over medium heat, and melt half the butter. Pour half of the batter into the skillet. Once the batter thickens up and looks mostly cooked and is brown on the edges, carefully flip it with a spatula. Remove from the skillet and onto a plate or cooling rack, then add the remaining butter and the remaining batter and repeat the cooking process.

Allow to cool for about 15 minutes, then place your favorite ingredients on top and roll the "bread" so it makes one big wrap. Cut into slices that are 1-inch (2.5 cm) thick for pinwheels.

YIELD: about 12 pinwheels

RAW COCONUT ALMOND BONBONS

With the perfect touch of sweetness, these bonbons are made with low-glycemic sweeteners that keep blood sugar levels stable and cravings at bay. The wholesome healthy fats help nourish your brain and keep you full and satisfied for hours on end. And with more antioxidants than green tea, the cacao will provide a boost of energy. But be sure not to eat these too late in the day if you are very sensitive to caffeine because they do contain small amounts.

1 cup (145 g) raw almonds

1 cup (80 g) unsweetened coconut flakes, divided

¾ cup (255 g) coconut nectar

½ cup (130 g) almond butter or peanut butter

½ cup (64 g) ground flaxseed meal

⅓ cup (27 g) raw cacao powder

3 tablespoons (36 g) coconut palm sugar

1 teaspoon vanilla extract

¼ teaspoon sea salt, if almond butter is unsalted

In a food processor, add the almonds, ⅔ cup (53 g) of the coconut flakes, coconut nectar, almond butter, flaxseed meal, cacao powder, coconut palm sugar, vanilla, and salt (if using). Process until a ball forms and everything is blended. With your hands, roll into golf ball–size balls. Take each ball and roll it in the remaining ⅓ cup (27 g) coconut flakes. Store in the fridge. Keep in a cooler for road trips, as they will stay together better if cool. But you can store in a small (so they aren't rolling around) airtight container if they are going to be consumed within a couple of hours of taking them out of the fridge.

YIELD: about 12 bonbons

STRAWBERRY GUMMIES

While these gummies are so fun to eat, they also have gelatin, which is a superfood. Shhh, don't tell the kiddos. The amino acids in gelatin help build muscle, aid in digestion, reduce joint pain, and support skin, hair, and nail growth. And it's a good source of protein and collagen. Yep, collagen, the stuff that makes skin tighter and reduces wrinkles. Who said these were just for the kids? This recipe works with most other fruits (except pineapple, papaya, and kiwi), so feel free to get creative.

2½ cups (365 g) strawberries, fresh or frozen and thawed

½ cup (120 ml) fresh lemon juice

2 tablespoons (40 g) raw honey

½ cup (72 g) grass-fed gelatin

Place the berries, lemon juice, and honey in a small saucepan and heat over low-medium heat. Cook until the fruit starts to soften. Then use an immersion blender (or allow to cool slightly before using a traditional blender) to purée the fruit.

Whisk in the gelatin a little at a time (so it won't clump up). Once you've stirred in all of the gelatin, pour the liquid into candy or ice cube silicon molds or into a 9 × 3-inch (23 × 33 cm) baking dish lined with parchment paper.

Place the gummies in the fridge for about 2 hours, until they congeal. Once done, pull them from the molds or slice them using a cookie cutter, pizza cutter, or knife. Store them in an airtight container either in the fridge or at room temperature.

They will last for 3 to 4 days at room temperature and a couple of weeks in the fridge.

YIELD: about 30 gummies

CINNAMON BUN BISCUITS

These buns are dense and chewy, and taste absolutely heavenly. Because they are full of fiber from the psyllium husk and good fats from the almond flour and butter, they will fill you up quickly and keep you satiated for hours.

For the biscuits:

- 2 cups (224 g) almond flour
- 1 cup (128 g) arrowroot powder
- ½ cup (96 g) coconut palm sugar
- 2 tablespoons (14 g) cinnamon
- 2 teaspoons (5 g) psyllium husk powder
- 1 teaspoon sea salt
- 2 eggs
- ¼ cup (85 g) maple syrup
- 2 tablespoons (28 g) grass-fed butter, melted

For the icing (optional):

- ¼ cup (55 g) coconut butter, melted
- 2 tablespoons (28 ml) almond milk or unsweetened canned coconut milk (stirred first)
- 1 tablespoon (20 g) maple syrup
- 1 teaspoon vanilla extract

Preheat the oven to 350°F (180°C, or gas mark 4). Line a baking sheet with parchment paper.

To make the biscuits: In a medium bowl, combine the almond flour, arrowroot powder, coconut palm sugar, cinnamon, psyllium husk powder, and salt. Add the eggs, maple syrup, and butter and mix well. Use your hands to make 8 roundish 2-inch (5 cm) balls and set on the prepared baking sheet. Bake for 15 minutes, or until a toothpick inserted in the middle of a biscuit comes out clean.

To make the optional icing: While the biscuits are baking, in a small microwave-safe bowl, stir together the coconut butter, almond milk, maple syrup, and vanilla. Heat in the microwave for about 40 seconds and stir until the mixture is smooth. Then as soon as the biscuits come out of the oven, apply the icing on top of the biscuits and let it cool just long enough so you don't burn your mouth, and then devour. If the frosting has hardened before the biscuits are ready, reheat for about 20 seconds.

YIELD: 8 biscuits

CHOCOLATE CHIP MUFFINS

These moist and delicious little snacks will not only satisfy your taste buds but will also keep you feeling full thanks to an abundance of healthy fats. Because they are made with low-glycemic sweeteners and a little caffeine (thank you, chocolate), these muffins will recharge your batteries—without the big sugar spike and trough associated with most sweet snacks. As with most recipes in this book, try to set your eggs out ahead of time so they can warm to room temperature. Otherwise, the chill from the eggs will solidify the coconut oil and can make the batter clumpy.

3 eggs, at room temperature

½ teaspoon vanilla extract

1 cup (260 g) smooth almond butter

1 cup (112 g) almond flour

½ cup (96 g) coconut palm sugar

⅓ cup (72 g) coconut oil, melted

½ teaspoon baking soda

¼ teaspoon sea salt

½ cup (88 g) dark chocolate chips

Preheat the oven to 350°F (180°C, or gas mark 4). Line a 12-cup muffin pan with silicone or paper muffin liners, or grease the cups.

In a small bowl, beat the eggs and then add in the vanilla. In a medium bowl, mix together the almond butter, almond flour, coconut palm sugar, coconut oil, baking soda, and salt. Add the egg mixture and stir until well combined. Fold in the chocolate chips.

Pour the batter into the prepared muffin cups about two-thirds full. Bake for 20 minutes, or until a toothpick inserted in the middle of a muffin comes out clean. Cool slightly before removing the muffins from the pan.

YIELD: 12 muffins

CINNAMON RAISIN BARS

Reminiscent of old-school cinnamon raisin bread, this delicious and easy-to-eat snack is perfect for the car. It can also be made nut-free by substituting almond butter with a sunflower seed butter and leaving out the walnuts (or substituting with dark chocolate chips).

4 eggs

1 cup (260 g) creamy almond butter or sunflower seed butter

1/3 cup (115 g) maple syrup

2 tablespoons (28 g) grass-fed butter, melted

2 tablespoons (24 g) coconut palm sugar

2 tablespoons (14 g) cinnamon

1 teaspoon vanilla extract

1/2 teaspoon baking soda

1/2 teaspoon sea salt

1/2 cup (35 g) raisins or currants

1/2 cup (25 g) walnuts (optional)

Preheat the oven to 325°F (170°C, or gas mark 3). Grease an 8 x 8-inch (20 x 20 cm) baking dish with coconut oil or palm shortening.

In a large bowl, combine the eggs, almond butter, maple syrup, butter, coconut palm sugar, cinnamon, vanilla, baking soda, and salt and stir until smooth. Fold in the raisins and walnuts, if using. Pour the batter into the prepared baking dish and move the dish around to ensure the batter is even. Bake for 25 minutes, or until a toothpick inserted in the middle of the bars comes out clean. Allow to cool for 30 minutes before cutting into bars and enjoying.

YIELD: 16 bars

MINI ZUCCHINI MUFFINS

These fun, supertasty, and easy-to-eat mini muffins are like little shots of omega-3 for your brain. Studies have shown omega-3s can increase happiness and relaxation. And who couldn't use a little more of that while on the road?

1 cup (112 g) almond flour

1 cup (128 g) flaxseed meal

1/3 cup (64 g) coconut palm sugar

1½ teaspoons (3.5 g) cinnamon

½ teaspoon sea salt

½ teaspoon baking soda

2 eggs

¼ cup (55 g) grass-fed butter, melted

½ cup (60 g) chopped raw walnuts

1/3 cup (50 g) currants or raisins

1 cup (124 g) peeled and grated zucchini (about 2 medium)

Preheat the oven to 350°F (180°C, or gas mark 4). Grease 32 cups of two 24-cup or one 48-cup mini-muffin pans.

In a medium bowl, mix the almond flour, flaxseed meal, coconut palm sugar, cinnamon, salt, and baking soda. In a small bowl, beat the eggs, and then add in the melted butter, walnuts, and raisins. Add the wet ingredients to the dry and mix until well blended. Then mix in the zucchini until combined.

Scoop the batter into the prepared muffin cups about three-quarters full. Bake for 25 minutes, or until a toothpick inserted in the middle of a muffin comes out clean.

YIELD: 32 mini muffins

ENERGY-REPLENISHING SNACKS

Pre- and Postworkout Foods That Provide Quick Fuel and Fast Recovery

When it comes to maximizing workout performance and recovery, knowing what to eat can be a huge challenge—a challenge made even more difficult by an onslaught of massive and misleading marketing campaigns aimed at connecting high-fructose sports drinks and soy-filled power bars with exercise benefits. These prepackaged options are more likely to yield an energy crash than to help performance during a workout. Worse, these "energy" snacks can cause deeper inflammation-related issues that could delay recovery and increase the chances of injury.

The pre-exercise snacks in this chapter are formulated with optimized ingredients that—when ingested about an hour before activity—provide energy for peak performance and aid in muscle reparation after exercise. Requirements are as follows:

CARBOHYDRATES

Paleo-safe carbohydrates restore glycogen levels in your muscles and get them ready for the next workout. Carbs, including sweet potatoes, bananas, and honey, quickly replace the energy stores you've depleted during the day and can be used immediately for extra energy.

FATS

Contrary to popular belief, fats actually play a more important role in exercise than carbohydrates do. According to the American Council on Exercise, approximately 60 percent of the calories you consume in lower-intensity aerobic exercise come from fat. Healthy fats—such as those found in almonds, cashews, and coconuts—are great sources of energy for the body. Powerful fats such as coconut oil are digested immediately to quickly produce energy and help stimulate metabolism, which in turn can enhance exercise performance.

PROTEIN

Protein helps supply our bodies with amino acids, which are building blocks for our muscle fibers. Amino acids slow the process of muscle breakdown when you are working out, help repair your muscles during recovery, and reduce muscle soreness. Research has shown that a mixture of proteins and carbohydrates taken before or after strenuous exercise effectively stimulates muscle repair after exercise.

SNACKING FOR WORKOUTS

Should you eat before, during, or after exercise?

- *Preworkout.* Unless you're still full from a previous meal, 30-60 minutes prior to the workout, you should eat a small (100- to 200-calorie) snack. This will help provide fuel for immediate energy, maintain blood sugar levels (giving you a more stable supply of energy), and assist in muscle recovery after exercise.
- *During Workout.* If you are an endurance athlete who works out for stints longer than 90 minutes at a time, a mouthful or two of a high-protein snack 60 minutes into the workout will help keep you from bonking or "hitting the wall."
- *Postworkout.* Research suggests that the key nutrients from preworkout snacks are still present enough in the body that you can skip the postworkout snack. However, if you didn't ingest a preworkout snack or exercised intensely for more than 90 minutes, you will need a snack after your workout. Eat within 30 minutes of your workout to ensure the right nutrients get back into your bloodstream so your body can begin to immediately repair muscles.

SWEET POTATO POWER BROWNIES

If you ever needed a reason to work out, this preworkout snack is it! These brownies are light, fluffy, and sweet. With the perfect combination of carbohydrates, fat, and protein, as well as a little kick of energy from the cacao, this snack is not only great for your workout but will also help assist you in a quick recovery.

2 medium sweet potatoes

6 eggs

2/3 cup (53 g) raw cacao powder

1/2 cup (170 g) raw honey or maple syrup

1/2 cup (130 g) almond butter

1/2 cup (56 g) almond flour

1/4 cup (55 g) plus 2 tablespoons (28 g), or 3/8 cup, grass-fed butter, softened

1/4 cup (48 g) coconut palm sugar

2 teaspoons (10 ml) vanilla extract

1 teaspoon baking soda

1/2 teaspoon sea salt

Preheat the oven to 400°F (200°C, or gas mark 6). Bake the sweet potatoes until soft, about 1 hour. When cool enough to handle, peel and mash. You should have about 2 cups (450 g). Reduce the heat to 350°F (180°C, or gas mark 4) and grease a 9 × 13-inch (23 × 33 cm) baking dish.

Place the sweet potatoes, eggs, cacao powder, honey, almond butter, almond flour, butter, coconut palm sugar, vanilla, baking soda, and salt in a food processor and blend well. (You may also use a hand mixer in a large bowl.) Spread the mixture into the prepared baking dish and bake for about 30 minutes. They are done when a toothpick inserted in the middle comes out clean.

Once they have cooled for a few minutes, cut into squares and refrigerate. They can be stored in the freezer as well.

YIELD: about 24 brownies

BANANA-BLUEBERRY POWER SQUARES

These sweet, fruit-filled bars provide some quick-burning fuel from the bananas and long-lasting energy from the honey and almond butter. Healthier than a typical workout bar, but loaded with antioxidants and protein, which is essential to build stronger muscles and to help your muscles recover properly, power squares really are, well, powerful.

Coconut oil

2 very ripe bananas

2 eggs

½ cup (130 g) smooth almond butter

½ cup (56 g) coconut flour

⅓ cup (115 g) dark raw honey

¼ cup (60 ml) unsweetened canned coconut milk (stirred first)

2 teaspoons (10 ml) vanilla extract

½ teaspoon cinnamon

¼ teaspoon baking soda

¼ teaspoon sea salt

¾ cup (109 g) fresh or frozen blueberries

Preheat the oven to 350°F (180°C, or gas mark 4). Grease an 8 x 8-inch (20 x 20 cm) baking dish with coconut oil.

In a food processor, blend together the bananas, eggs, almond butter, coconut flour, honey, coconut milk, vanilla, cinnamon, baking soda, and salt until well combined. Fold in the blueberries. (If using frozen blueberries, place them in a colander and run them under hot water to thaw them before folding them into the mixture.) Pour the mixture into the prepared baking dish. Bake for 45 minutes, or until a toothpick inserted in the middle comes out clean. Allow to cool for 15 minutes before cutting into squares.

YIELD: sixteen 2-inch (5 cm) squares

CHERRY-CACAO ENERGY BALLS

This is a great snack to help you fuel up for a long endurance event. I even pack a few of these if I'm going on a long run or bike ride. The cacao gives a little boost of energy, and the honey is perfect for muscle stamina.

1 cup (145 g) raw almonds

½ cup (96 g) coconut palm sugar

3 tablespoons (15 g) raw cacao powder

Dash of sea salt

¼ cup (85 g) dark raw honey

¼ cup (65 g) smooth almond butter

⅓ cup (42 g) dried cherries

In a food processor, process the almonds until they are in small pieces. Transfer them to a medium bowl and mix together with the coconut palm sugar, cacao powder, and salt. Add the honey, almond butter, and cherries to the bowl and use your hands to mash together well. Form firm golf ball–size balls. Store in an airtight container on your countertop, fridge, or freezer for a cool treat.

YIELD: about 12 balls

CRUNCHY GRANOLA BRITTLE

These bars have the crunchy goodness of traditional granola bars, but without inflammation-causing grains, sugar, or soy flour. With a little shot of honey to help improve endurance and stabilize your blood sugar, this really is a supreme energy bar. Feel free to substitute 2 cups (300 g) of your favorite assortment of nuts and seeds.

½ cup (73 g) almonds
½ cup (55 g) cashews
½ cup (113 g) pepitas
½ cup (82 g) chia seeds
¼ cup (44 g) flaxseeds
1 teaspoon cinnamon
½ teaspoon sea salt
1 cup (340 g) raw honey
1 teaspoon vanilla extract

Preheat the oven to 350°F (180°C, or gas mark 4). Line a baking sheet with parchment paper.

In a food processor, lightly chop the almonds and cashews. Then add in the pepitas, chia seeds, flaxseeds, cinnamon, and salt. Pulse until well combined.

In a small saucepan over medium-low heat, combine the honey and vanilla. You want to heat it just long enough (4 to 5 minutes) to reduce the viscosity so that it will be easy to combine with the nuts and seeds. Pour the honey mixture into the food processor and pulse a few more times to mix everything together.

Spread the granola mixture over the prepared baking sheet so the granola is about ½-inch (1.5 cm) thick. Lay another piece of parchment paper over the top and press down firmly and evenly. Remove the top layer of parchment and bake for 10 minutes. Remove from the oven, add back the top layer of parchment, and carefully flip the granola over, setting it back onto the baking sheet. Once flipped, remove the top layer of parchment and bake for an additional 5 to 7 minutes, or until it is golden brown. Allow it to cool for 1 hour so it can harden. Break apart and eat!

YIELD: about 8 servings

HONEY ALMOND NUT BUTTER

If you've ever watched or participated in a marathon or triathlon, you may be familiar with the concept of GU, an easy-to-digest, high-protein snack athletes consume while on the course. I've found a more whole-food and natural alternative with homemade Honey Almond Nut Butter. This easy-to-eat energy shot is a great source of quick fuel and perfect for recovery, as well.

1 cup (145 g) almonds, soaked and roasted or dehydrated (see page 22)

1 tablespoon (20 g) raw honey

1 teaspoon coconut oil

1 teaspoon sea salt

¼ teaspoon vanilla extract

In a food processor or blender, blend the almonds, honey, coconut oil, salt, and vanilla on medium speed. Do not try to blend it on high or it will not form properly. Your mixture will be powdery at first but then start to solidify after 2 to 3 minutes. Store in an airtight container in the fridge for up to 4 weeks.

This is great on fruit, some gluten-free crackers, or alone. Alternatively, use a sandwich bag and place the nut butter in one of the bottom corners. Then, twist the bag so the almond butter is concentrated together in one corner. When you are ready for it, just tear off that corner and squeeze it into your mouth, like you would with GU.

YIELD: about ½ cup (130 g)

BANANA NUT BITES

These unpretentious little bites are crispy on the outside and sweet and chewy on the inside and are bursting with flavor. Not only are bananas the perfect preworkout carbohydrate, but they are also full of potassium, which helps stave off cramps and aids in the postworkout rebuilding of muscles.

2 or 3 very ripe bananas

2 cups (290 g) almonds

2 tablespoons (16 g) flaxseed meal

1 teaspoon cinnamon

1 cup (340 g) raw honey

⅓ cup (75 g) grass-fed butter

Preheat the oven to 350°F (180°C, or gas mark 4). Line a baking sheet with parchment paper.

In a small bowl, mash the bananas with a fork. You should have about 1 cup (225 g). Blend the almonds in the food processor until they are broken up into tiny pieces. Then add the flaxseed meal and cinnamon and blend for a few more seconds. In a small saucepan over medium-low heat, melt the honey and butter. Pour the honey mixture and the bananas into the food processor and blend everything together until it's well combined.

Scoop out the mixture with a tablespoon and place it on the baking sheet. Leave about 1 inch (2.5 cm) in between each bite, because they won't expand like a traditional cookie. Repeat with the remaining dough. Bake for 14 to 17 minutes, or until a toothpick inserted in the middle of a bite comes out clean.

YIELD: 30 bites

POWERHOUSE PALEO COFFEE

Many studies link caffeine intake before a workout to improved performance and focus. Add a banana for quick-burning carbs, some honey and chia seeds to help increase your endurance and balance blood sugar levels, and coconut water to rehydrate you better than any sports drink, and you have the perfect workout drink.

¾ cup (175 ml) cold coffee

¼ cup (60 ml) almond milk

1 tablespoon (10 g) chia seeds

1 tablespoon (5 g) raw cacao powder

1½ teaspoons (10 g) raw honey

1 frozen banana

6 coconut water ice cubes

In a blender, blend the coffee, almond milk, chia seeds, cacao powder, honey, banana, and ice cubes for about 1 minute, or until it is a milkshake-like consistency. Yum.

If you make and chill the coffee (just save some in the fridge from breakfast time) and freeze the coconut water and banana ahead of time, this drink is quick and easy to prepare. If you don't have an ice cube tray for the coconut water, you can use a muffin pan instead. Simply freeze ½ cup (120 ml) coconut water between 2 muffin pans.

YIELD: 1 large serving

CHOCOLATE CHIA WORKOUT BARS

Often referred to as a "superfood" for good reason, chia seeds are a fantastic source of energy for a workout. They digest easily and are absorbed quickly. Just a few bites of these tasty bars will give you a boost of power and keep you sustained for the duration of your activity. Be forewarned: You might not want to eat these too late in the day as the cacao powder might give you too much energy!

- 1 cup (220 g) coconut butter
- ⅓ cup (115 g) dark raw honey
- ½ cup (113 g) salted and roasted sunflower seeds
- ½ cup (82 g) chia seeds
- ⅓ cup (27 g) raw cacao powder
- ¼ cup (20 g) unsweetened shredded coconut
- ¼ cup (44 g) dark chocolate chips
- ¼ teaspoon sea salt

In a small saucepan over low heat, melt the coconut butter and honey. While that is warming up, in a medium bowl, mix together the sunflower seeds, chia seeds, cacao powder, coconut, chocolate chips, and salt. When the liquids are melted, about 5 minutes, pour them over the dry ingredients and stir well. Pour the mixture onto a baking sheet lined with parchment paper. Use another piece of parchment paper to flatten the mixture to about ¼-inch (6 mm) thick, then refrigerate for 1 hour. Once it has solidified, cut into bars. Store in the fridge or freezer.

YIELD: about 12 bars

CRUNCHY SWEET POTATO FRIES

These are a longtime staple of my diet and a favorite preworkout snack. With just a little prep work, this snack is simple to make. The key is to keep a bag of precut sweet potatoes in the fridge and then just bake and serve. They are great with plenty of coarse sea salt, which is perfect for topping up minerals in your body that are lost during a sweaty workout.

1 large sweet potato

2 tablespoons (16 g) arrowroot powder

2 to 3 tablespoons (27 g) coconut oil, melted

Coarse sea salt

Cinnamon

Preheat the oven to 425°F (220°C, or gas mark 7).

Use a mandolin slicer to cut the potato into medallions about ⅛ inch (3 mm) thick. You can also use a knife to cut them into a traditional french fry shape (or medallions). Place the potatoes in a quart-size (1 L) resealable plastic bag, add the arrowroot powder, close the bag, and shake so the arrowroot fully coats the potatoes.

Lay the potatoes out flat on a baking sheet (without parchment paper). Drizzle with coconut oil and bake for 20 minutes. Turn and cook for another 5 to 10 minutes, until crispy. Sprinkle with salt and cinnamon. Allow to cool long enough so you won't burn your mouth, then devour.

YIELD: 3 or 4 servings

CHOCOLATE BANANA SMOOTHIE

If you tend to have a nervous stomach prior to races or a big game, blending foods may provide you with a more easily digestible snack. This delicious smoothie has the right balance of potassium and carbohydrates to prep you for a workout, and it will keep you satiated.

1 cup (235 ml) unsweetened canned light coconut milk or almond milk

1 very ripe banana

2 to 3 tablespoons (32 to 48 g) almond butter or any nut/seed butter

1 tablespoon (5 g) raw cacao powder (optional)

Small handful of ice

1 tablespoon (11 g) dark chocolate chips

Place the coconut milk, banana, almond butter, cacao powder, and ice into a blender and blend on high speed until smooth. Add in the chocolate chips and pulse 5 to 10 times.

YIELD: 1 large serving

TIP: Double the recipe and put the remaining smoothie in ice pop holders to freeze for another time.

BANANA WALNUT MUFFINS

With a light buttery flavor, these supermoist muffins will melt in your mouth. They are a fantastic source of healthy fat, fiber, and protein, which will help keep you going strong through an extended workout. The only problem is, it is hard to eat just one. Good thing they are healthy!

---

2 or 3 very ripe bananas

½ cup (112 g) grass-fed butter, melted

4 eggs

½ cup (56 g) almond flour

½ cup (56 g) coconut flour

⅓ cup (64 g) coconut palm sugar

¼ cup (25 g) walnuts, finely chopped

¾ teaspoon baking soda

¾ teaspoon cinnamon

½ teaspoon vanilla extract

Pinch of sea salt

Preheat the oven to 350°F (180°C, or gas mark 4). Line a 12-cup muffin pan with silicone or paper muffin liners, or grease the cups.

In a mixing bowl, mash the bananas well with a fork. You should have about 1 cup (225 g). Add the butter and then stir in the eggs, almond flour, coconut flour, coconut palm sugar, walnuts, baking soda, cinnamon, vanilla, and salt. Stir until you have a nice smooth consistency. Pour the batter into the prepared muffin cups about two-thirds full. Bake for 20 minutes, or until a toothpick inserted in the center of a muffin comes out clean.

YIELD: 12 muffins

SWEET POTATO CASSEROLE BREAD

No need to wait until Thanksgiving to have a delicious sweet potato casserole! This mouth-drooling portable snack is a great source of energy for your workout. With a full cup of nutrient-rich complex carbohydrates and muscle-building minerals from the sweet potato and almonds, this bread will help you perform your best.

1½ cups (168 g) almond flour

1 cup (192 g) plus 1 tablespoon (12 g) coconut palm sugar or dark raw honey, divided

½ cup (56 g) coconut flour

2 tablespoons (14 g) cinnamon

2 teaspoons (5 g) nutmeg

1 teaspoon baking soda

½ teaspoons sea salt

6 eggs

1 cup (225 g) cooked and mashed sweet potato

2 teaspoons (10 ml) vanilla

¼ cup (25 g) pecans, chopped

Preheat the oven to 350°F (180°C, or gas mark 4). Grease a 5 × 9-inch (13 × 23 cm) loaf pan.

In a medium bowl, mix together the almond flour, 1 cup (192 g) of the coconut palm sugar, coconut flour, cinnamon, nutmeg, baking soda, and salt. In a small bowl, beat the eggs with a spoon or hand mixer. Add the sweet potato and vanilla and mix until well combined. Add the wet ingredients to the dry and mix together until smooth and no lumps are left. Pour the mixture into the prepared pan. Make the topping by mixing together the pecans and remaining 1 tablespoon (12 g) coconut palm sugar, and spread evenly over the top of the bread. Bake for 50 to 60 minutes, or until a toothpick inserted in the middle of the loaf comes out clean. Allow to cool in the pan for 20 minutes before slicing.

YIELD: 8 to 10 servings

BACON & SWEET POTATO HASH

This ideal workout starch is made into a versatile snack that is delicious alone or with eggs, guacamole, ground beef, sausage . . . you name it. Make a batch of it on Sunday and you'll be set to go all week!

2 large sweet potatoes

6 slices nitrate-free bacon, cut into bite-size pieces

1 onion, chopped

1 teaspoon garlic powder

1 teaspoon onion powder

1 teaspoon chili powder

1 teaspoon sea salt

¼ teaspoon cayenne pepper

1 tablespoon (20 g) maple syrup (optional)

Peel the sweet potatoes and then shred in a food processor. In a large skillet over medium heat, cook the bacon until crispy, 8 to 10 minutes, and then set the bacon aside on a plate lined with a paper towel.

In the bacon grease, sauté the onion over medium to medium-high heat until it starts to brown, about 5 minutes. Add in the sweet potatoes and cook, stirring every few minutes, until the potatoes are soft and starting to brown, about 15 minutes. Once they are done, add in the garlic powder, onion powder, chili powder, salt, cayenne, maple syrup (if using), and bacon bits. Serve with scrambled eggs, ground beef, sausage, avocado, or whatever you'd like to make the perfect recovery meal!

YIELD: 8 servings

CHOCOLATE MUFFINS

This is a perfect snack for the chocolate lover. Loaded with powerful antioxidants, it can help improve mood as well as help us deal with pain, thanks to its serotonin-boosting power. Make sure your eggs are at room temperature; otherwise, the coconut oil will solidify and the batter might be hard to combine.

½ cup (56 g) almond flour

½ cup (56 g) coconut flour

⅓ cup (27 g) raw cacao powder

¾ teaspoon baking soda

Pinch of sea salt

4 eggs, at room temperature

½ cup (170 g) dark raw honey

1 teaspoon vanilla extract

½ cup (108 g) coconut oil, melted

¼ cup (44 g) mini chocolate chips for the top

Preheat the oven to 350°F (180°C, or gas mark 4). Line a 12-cup muffin pan with silicone or paper muffin liners, or grease the cups.

In a medium bowl, mix together the almond flour, coconut flour, cacao powder, baking soda, and salt. In a small bowl, whisk the eggs, and then whisk in the honey and vanilla and combine well. Add the wet ingredients to the dry and mix well. Add the coconut oil and stir until it's smooth. Fill each muffin cup about two-thirds full and sprinkle the chocolate chips on top. Bake for 20 minutes, or until a toothpick inserted in the middle of a muffin comes out clean.

YIELD: 12 muffins

CHIA PUDDING

I recommend making this pudding the night before your workout so it can thicken. Keep it in your fridge and then before heading out for your activity, eat a few big spoonfuls and you'll be good to go. There's no muss or fuss, it's easy to eat, and it's great for fueling your workout.

1 cup (235 ml) almond milk or unsweetened canned coconut milk (stirred first)

½ cup (82 g) chia seeds

¼ cup (85 g) dark raw honey

1 tablespoon (5 g) raw cacao powder

1 teaspoon cinnamon

½ teaspoon vanilla extract

Blueberries and slivered almonds, for topping (optional)

Mix together the almond milk, chia seeds, honey, cacao powder, cinnamon, and vanilla. Let sit for an hour, or overnight, and top with blueberries and slivered almonds, if desired, just before serving. Store in a mason jar for easy access and good storage. It will last in the fridge for 3 or 4 days.

YIELD: 1 large serving

SWEET POTATO PANCAKES

When working out, it is really important to find the right balance of carbs and proteins. These superdelicious pancakes certainly fit the bill. They are great alone, but I love to add a little Honey Almond Nut Butter (page 133) or Chocolate Sunflower Seed Butter (page 157). Both your taste buds and your muscles will thank you.

1 cup (225 g) mashed cooked sweet potato (about 2 small sweet potatoes)

4 eggs

¼ cup (28 g) almond or cashew flour

2 tablespoons (40 g) dark raw honey or maple syrup

1 teaspoon cinnamon

¼ teaspoon baking soda

¼ teaspoon vanilla extract

1 tablespoon (13.5 g) coconut oil

In a medium bowl, mix the sweet potato, eggs, almond flour, honey, cinnamon, baking soda, and vanilla with an immersion blender, or use a food processor, to ensure that the sweet potato is smooth.

In a large pan over medium-high heat, melt the coconut oil. Pour the mixture into pancakes about 4 inches (10 cm) in diameter. Cook for about 3 minutes, until they become golden brown. Turn, then cook for another 3 minutes, or until light brown.

YIELD: 8 to 10 pancakes

NUT-FREE SNACKS

*Scrumptious Paleo Snacks without Tree Nuts
or Peanuts*

Nuts are a delicious, nutritious, and convenient snack. They are also a staple of the Paleo diet. But for individuals with nut allergies, embracing Paleo can be a real challenge.

Yet it doesn't have to be that way. In this chapter I've pulled together some of my favorite nut-free snacks that will allow you to enjoy your granola, bars, raw bites, and other snacks that are traditionally made with nuts, but without the worry of these high-allergen ingredients.

Let's face it: Nut allergies are on the rise. According to a FARE (Food Allergy Research & Education)–funded study, the number of children in the United States with a peanut allergy more than tripled between 1997 and 2008. Even more concerning is how life-threatening these allergies can be. In an effort to protect children, many schools have instituted nut-free classrooms and sections of the lunchroom. Workplaces are following suit. Whether or not a nut allergy affects you directly, it's likely you will face a time when you need to prepare nut-free snacks for yourself, your kids, or others.

With the recipes in this chapter, you can be confident and rest assured. I have consulted with and shopped for individuals with severe nut allergies for whom ingesting the slightest trace of nuts can be deadly. Surprisingly, when shopping for ingredients, it can be challenging to determine whether nut cross-contamination might be present. If you are not accustomed to preparing foods for someone with an allergy, be sure to check labels for notes such as "manufactured in a facility that also produces nuts." When in doubt, call the manufacturer to be sure.

One of the best things about preparing your own snacks is the worry-free confidence you gain by knowing that what you serve is made with safe ingredients. What's more, being nut-free doesn't mean you have to skimp on protein or healthy fats.

This chapter uses a number of delicious and beneficial nut-free alternative ingredients. Pumpkin seeds (also known as pepitas) are high in minerals and have the highest concentration of iron of any nonanimal source. Sunflower seeds, in addition to being both low-carb and low-glycemic, contain an abundance of vitamin E and selenium, which is essential for optimal thyroid function. Of course, chia seeds and flaxseeds are a terrific source of fiber and omega-3s. Most important, these ingredients have a perfect crunchy texture and satisfying taste. After all, just because a recipe is nut-free doesn't mean that it has to be taste-free.

PUMPKIN-SPICED GRANOLA BARS

This supertasty nut-free bar is one of the most nutritionally dense granola bars. The protein in the bar will help keep blood sugar levels stable and keep you full for long periods of time. It also has zinc, which is great for keeping immune systems strong, and magnesium to help with migraines—and even lift moods. And with lots of healthy oils, specifically omega-3s, this delectable bar can also help reduce inflammation.

2 cups (450 g) raw pepitas

1 cup (80 g) unsweetened shredded coconut

1 cup (125 g) dried unsweetened cherries or blueberries, chopped

¼ cup (44 g) whole flaxseeds

¼ cup (41 g) chia seeds

1 teaspoon pumpkin pie spice

1 teaspoon ground cinnamon

¼ teaspoon sea salt

½ cup (123 g) canned pumpkin purée

1 cup (340 g) coconut nectar or raw honey

3 tablespoons (40 g) coconut oil

1 teaspoon vanilla extract

Preheat the oven to 275°F (140°C, or gas mark 1). Line a 9 × 13-inch (23 × 33 cm) jelly-roll pan with parchment paper.

In a large bowl, stir together the pepitas, coconut, cherries, flaxseeds, chia seeds, pumpkin pie spice, cinnamon, and salt. Then add the pumpkin and stir as best you can.

In a small saucepan over medium heat, whisk together the coconut nectar, coconut oil, and vanilla and bring to a slight boil. Remove from the heat and pour the liquid mixture over the dry ingredients with the pumpkin and mix together. Pour the mixture onto the prepared baking sheet. With another piece of parchment paper on top, press down firmly until you have a flat, even thickness, about ½ inch (1.5 cm) thick. Remove the top layer of parchment and bake for 30 to 35 minutes, or until the bars start to harden. Remove from the oven and let cool completely. Refrigerate for an hour or so before cutting into bars. Store in the fridge.

YIELD: 16 to 18 bars

APPLE PIE TRAIL MIX BALLS

This fun trail mix wrapped up into a nut-free apple ball is similar to some store-bought bars, but without all of the dates (that so many Paleo-friendly bars use) or sugar. Because these balls are made with low-glycemic sugars, you won't have those crazy blood sugar swings or crashes.

1 cup (225 g) raw pepitas

1/3 cup (about 12 rings) unsweetened dried apples

1/4 cup (48 g) coconut palm sugar

1/4 cup (85 g) coconut nectar

1/4 cup (65 g) sunflower seed butter

2 tablespoons (10 g) unsweetened shredded coconut

1 teaspoon cinnamon

Dash of sea salt

In a food processor, blend the pepitas until they are in small pieces. Add in the apples, coconut palm sugar, coconut nectar, sunflower seed butter, coconut, cinnamon, and salt and blend until everything starts to clump into one big ball. Remove the mixture from the processor. Using your hands, shape the dough into 12 balls about the size of golf balls. Place in the fridge for about 30 minutes to set.

YIELD: 12 balls

CRUNCHY OMEGA-3 FLAX GRANOLA

This yummy, ultracrispy, super granola is an easy way to get plenty of fiber and omega-3s that we need for maximum gut and hormonal health. This is great on its own or mixed with yogurt.

1 cup (176 g) whole flaxseeds

½ cup (113 g) raw pepitas

¼ cup (41 g) chia seeds

¼ cup (56 g) raw sunflower seeds

1 tablespoon (7 g) cinnamon

2 teaspoons (12 g) sea salt

¾ cup (175 ml) water

¼ cup (48 g) coconut palm sugar

½ cup (40 g) unsweetened shredded coconut

½ cup (75 g) dried fruit of choice

In a small bowl, mix the dry ingredients together. Then add the water, combine well, and let sit for 10 minutes.

Preheat the oven to 180°F (82°C). Line a baking sheet with parchment paper.

Spread the mixture as flat and evenly as possible on the prepared baking sheet. Bake for 8 to 10 hours or until crispy. Allow to cool for 30 minutes. Break apart and enjoy. Stored in an airtight container at room temperature, this granola will keep for a couple of weeks.

YIELD: about 3 cups (366 g)

"PEANUT BUTTER" PATTIES

Similar to a traditional Girl Scout Tag-A-Long peanut butter cookie, but without the peanuts or hydrogenated oil, this nut-free treat is a safe and delicious snack.

½ cup (112 g) grass-fed butter, melted (use palm shortening if allergic)

½ cup (170 g) raw honey

2 eggs

½ cup (56 g) coconut flour

3 tablespoons (24 g) arrowroot powder

Dash of sea salt

½ cup plus 2 teaspoons (140 g) sunflower seed butter

1 cup (175 g) dark chocolate chips

Preheat the oven to 350°F (180°C, or gas mark 4). Line a baking sheet with parchment paper.

In a medium bowl, mix together the butter, honey, and eggs. In a small bowl, mix together the coconut flour, arrowroot, and salt. Pour the dry ingredients into the wet and mix well.

Spread the dough on a piece of parchment paper. Place another piece of parchment paper on top and flatten the dough with a rolling pin so it is about ⅛-inch (3 mm) thick. Use a circular cookie cutter to stamp out patties and set them on the prepared baking sheet with about 1 inch (2.5 cm) of space between them. Mash together the dough scraps and flatten it again so you can use it all.

Bake for 6 to 8 minutes, until they feel firm to the touch. Remove from the oven, and allow to cool on a baking rack for 1 hour. Once cool, spread 1 teaspoon of sunflower seed butter on the top of each cookie.

Meanwhile, add the chocolate chips to a heat-safe bowl and set the bowl over a small saucepan of simmering water (do not let the water touch the bowl). Melt the chocolate. Remove the bowl from the heat and stir until the chocolate is smooth. Allow the chocolate to cool for about 10 minutes before using on the cookies or else it will melt the sunflower seed butter.

Take a cookie and dip the top (sunflower seed butter side) face-down into the chocolate. Then, place back on the baking sheet to set. Store in the fridge or freezer.

YIELD: about 26 cookies

BEST NUT-FREE MUFFINS AROUND

They say the muffin tops are the best. In this case, the crispy tops are perfect with a sweet cookie-like taste and texture, but the ooey-gooey bottoms are just as divine. It's hard to say which is better, but together, it makes the perfect muffin. Alternatively, you can make just the muffin tops with this recipe, if that is what you prefer. (I think of them as cookies, the happy result after playing around with some extra batter.) Either way, these iron-packed treats are one of my favorite snacks.

1 cup (225 g) raw pepitas

½ cup (96 g) coconut palm sugar

¼ teaspoon baking soda (omit if making cookies)

⅛ teaspoon sea salt

¼ cup (55 g) grass-fed butter, melted

1 egg

1 teaspoon vanilla extract

⅓ cup (58 g) dark chocolate chips

¼ cup (56 g) roasted and salted sunflower seeds

Preheat the oven to 350°F (180°C, or gas mark 4). Line a 12-cup mini muffin pan with silicone or paper muffin liners, or grease the cups. (If making cookies, line a baking sheet with parchment paper.)

In a coffee grinder or food processor, grind the pepitas until they become a flour-like powder. In a medium bowl, mix together the ground pepitas, coconut palm sugar, baking soda (if using), and salt. In a small bowl, mix together the butter, egg, and vanilla. Pour the wet ingredients into the dry and mix well. Fold in the chocolate chips and sunflower seeds.

Pour the batter into the prepared muffin cups about three-quarters full. Bake for 11 minutes, or until a toothpick inserted into the center of a muffin comes out clean.

If you want to make cookies instead, spoon the mixture onto a prepared baking sheet and bake for 8 to 10 minutes, or until they start to brown and become somewhat crispy. The cookies are amazing, too!

YIELD: 12 mini muffins or 12 cookies

CHOCOLATE SUNFLOWER SEED BUTTER

You may not know what you are missing if you have never tried Nutella. It is one of the most popular snacks out there—and with good reason. Nutella is easy to eat as a snack topping. Unfortunately, while Nutella tastes good, it is full of sugar, and, of course, hazelnuts, which can clearly pose a problem for those with nut allergies. This much healthier, nut-free version (with soaked seeds for added benefit, if you prefer) is a fantastic spread on fruit or Flatbread "PB&J" (page 158). Or, just grab a spoon and start eating!

2 cups (450 g) roasted sunflower seeds

¼ cup (20 g) raw cacao powder

¼ teaspoon sea salt

⅓ cup (58 g) dark chocolate chips

3 tablespoons (60 g) maple syrup

3 tablespoons (41 g) coconut oil

2 tablespoons (28 g) coconut butter

1 tablespoon (15 ml) vanilla extract

In a food processor, blend the sunflower seeds, cacao powder, and salt. The mixture will be powdery at first and then it will thicken. It should take about 3 minutes to firm up.

In a small saucepan over medium heat, melt the chocolate chips, maple syrup, coconut oil, coconut butter, and vanilla extract. Then pour into the food processor with the sunflower seed mixture. Blend on medium speed until smooth. Enjoy it while it is warm, or store in an airtight container in the fridge. It should keep in the fridge for 6 to 8 weeks, if it lasts that long!

YIELD: about 1¾ cups (455 g)

FLATBREAD "PB&J"

This supertasty roll-up will let you enjoy a sandwich-like snack without the guilt or worry of eating a high-carb, gluten-filled, high-glycemic bread. It's great with sunflower seed butter and fresh cut-up strawberries or fruit of your choice, and you'll never have to miss sandwich bread . . . or the peanut butter or jelly, for that matter. This easy-to-roll snack will become one of your favorites, and the bread is a great staple for those who miss their "bread."

½ cup (56 g) coconut flour

2 tablespoons (16 g) psyllium husk powder

1 tablespoon (12 g) coconut palm sugar

1 teaspoon cinnamon

¼ cup (54 g) coconut oil

1 cup (235 ml) boiling water

⅓ cup (75 g) sunflower seed butter

10 strawberries, thinly sliced

Preheat the oven to 375°F (190°C, or gas mark 5). Line a baking sheet with parchment paper. In a medium bowl, mix together the coconut flour, psyllium husk powder, coconut palm sugar, and cinnamon. Add the coconut oil and hot water and stir it all together.

Spread the dough out on the prepared baking sheet. With a rolling pin or glass, flatten out the dough as evenly as you can so it's about ½-inch (1.5 cm) thick. Bake for 15 minutes, or until a toothpick inserted into the center comes out clean. Then move to a cooling rack and allow to cool to room temperature.

Once the dough is cool, spread on the sunflower seed butter and strawberries (or whatever fruit you would like). Then carefully roll the "bread" and slice, with a pizza cutter or knife, into 3-inch (7.5 cm) pieces.

YIELD: 5 sandwiches

CRISPY FOUR-SEED GRANOLA

This sweet, light, and crunchy granola is wonderful alone, or mixed with some coconut/almond milk and/or fresh fruit. We just love to eat it fresh from the oven by the spoonful. Be careful, though, it's additive—and you won't even notice it's missing nuts!

¾ cup (60 g) unsweetened shredded coconut

½ cup (113 g) raw sunflower seeds

½ cup (113 g) raw pepitas

⅓ cup (64 g) coconut palm sugar

2 tablespoons (22 g) raw flaxseeds

2 tablespoons (20 g) chia seeds

2 tablespoons (27 g) coconut oil

1 teaspoon cinnamon

¼ teaspoon sea salt

Preheat the oven to 350°F (180°C, or gas mark 4). Line a baking sheet with parchment paper.

In a medium bowl, mix together the coconut, sunflower seeds, pepitas, coconut palm sugar, flaxseeds, chia seeds, coconut oil, cinnamon, and salt. Spread evenly on the prepared baking sheet and bake for about 10 minutes, until it starts to brown. Allow it to cool for about 20 minutes. It will get crispier as it cools. Store in an airtight container.

YIELD: about 2 cups (244 g)

SWEET & SALTY SPICED PEPITAS

Pepitas are a wonderful snack because they are high in both iron and zinc, which are vital for enhancing memory, and great for strengthening your immune system and helping boost energy. Moreover, they have a perfect crunch. Add a little salt and a little sweetness and you have a fabulously addictive snack!

2 cups (450 g) raw pepitas

2 teaspoons (5 g) pumpkin pie spice

1 teaspoon sea salt

1½ tablespoons (30 g) maple syrup

Preheat the oven to 350°F (180°C, or gas mark 4). Line a baking sheet with parchment paper.

In a medium bowl, mix together the pepitas, pumpkin pie spice, and salt. Add in the maple syrup and stir until the pumpkin seed mixture is evenly coated. Spread out the seeds evenly on the prepared baking sheet and bake for 12 minutes, or until they start to turn brown, stirring halfway through so they bake evenly. Take out of the oven and allow to cool for at least 30 minutes. As they cool they will get even crunchier! Store in an airtight container.

YIELD: 2 cups (450 g)

"PEANUT BUTTER" COOKIES

Sunflower seeds have a similar makeup to that of peanuts. When it comes to oil, protein, and carbohydrate content, they're pretty close. The taste of these cookies is as close as you can get to a peanut butter cookie, and just as mouthwatering, but without the peanuts. Sunflower seeds are also considered to be one of the best whole-food sources of vitamin E, which helps protect brain cells and lowers the risk for chronic diseases. So now you have an excuse to eat even more of this rich, delectable treat!

2 cups (520 g) sunflower seed butter

1 cup (192 g) coconut palm sugar

1 tablespoon (15 ml) vanilla extract

¼ teaspoon sea salt

Preheat the oven to 350°F (180°C, or gas mark 4). Line a baking sheet with parchment paper.

In a medium bowl, mix together the sunflower seed butter, coconut palm sugar, vanilla extract, and salt and stir until well combined. Form golf ball–size pieces of dough and set on the prepared baking sheet. (Make sure the cookies have about 1 inch, or 2.5 cm, between them. You may have to use 2 baking sheets or bake in 2 batches.) Press the dough down to make the cookies a little flat and then use a fork to press a crisscross pattern onto them. Bake for 10 minutes, or until a toothpick inserted in the middle of a cookie comes out clean (they will not turn brown on top like traditional peanut butter cookies). Let cool. Enjoy!

YIELD: about 24 cookies

CHOCOLATE ZUCCHINI "BREAD"

It's almost hard to call this wonderful snack "bread" because there isn't any wheat and it tastes like a treat. Yet, its texture is amazing, and it's loaded with powerful antioxidants, which can stimulate the production of endorphins to help you feel great. And if the endorphins don't, the taste of this bread will!

1 cup (260 g) sunflower seed butter

½ cup (170 g) maple syrup

⅓ cup (27 g) raw cacao powder

2 eggs

1 tablespoon (15 ml) vanilla extract

2 teaspoons (10 ml) apple cider vinegar

½ teaspoon baking soda

⅛ teaspoon sea salt

1 zucchini (about ½ pound, or 225 g)

½ cup (88 g) dark chocolate chips

Preheat the oven to 400°F (200°C, or gas mark 6). Grease a 5 x 9-inch (13 x 23 cm) loaf pan.

In a medium bowl, combine the sunflower seed butter, maple syrup, cacao powder, eggs, vanilla, vinegar, baking soda, and salt and blend well.

Peel the zucchini and then shred or grate; you should have about 1 cup (124 g). Place on a paper towel. Using the towel, squeeze out the excess moisture from the zucchini. Add the zucchini and most of your chocolate chips (reserve about 2 tablespoons, or 22 g, for topping) to the mixture and stir well.

Pour the batter into the prepared loaf pan. Top with the remaining dark chocolate chips. Bake for 40 to 50 minutes, or until a toothpick inserted in the middle of the bread comes out clean. Store in an airtight container on the counter for 3 to 4 days, in the fridge for up to 7 days, or in the freezer for 30 days. Reheat in the microwave or toaster when ready to eat.

YIELD: 8 servings

PIZZA POCKETS

In my opinion, this is the best, tastiest, healthiest gluten-free pizza out there. They are fun and simple to make: create different varieties with your own favorite topping each time. And the best part is, they actually have a gluten-like texture (squishy bread), unlike any other gluten-free pizza, but without the gut-damaging effects. These yummy fiber-filled treats will keep you full for hours.

½ cup (56 g) coconut flour

2 tablespoons (16 g) psyllium husk powder

1 teaspoon dried oregano

1 teaspoon dried basil

¼ teaspoon sea salt

1 cup (235 ml) water

¼ cup (55 g) grass-fed butter

¼ to ½ cup (63 to 125 g) pizza sauce (such as Muir Glen, which comes in BPA-free cans) or tomato sauce

10 to 20 pepperoni (such as Wellshire uncured)

Preheat the oven 325°F (170°C, or gas mark 3). Line a baking sheet with parchment paper.

In a medium bowl, mix together the coconut flour, psyllium husk powder, oregano, basil, and salt. In a small saucepan, boil the water and add the butter. Cook until the butter is melted. Pour the water/butter into the bowl with the dry ingredients and mix well with a spoon. Once it starts to become dough-like, use your hands to knead it all together.

Set the dough on a piece of parchment paper. With another piece of parchment paper on top of the dough, flatten it with your hands. Then roll it out with a rolling pin. Try to get it as thin as possible (about ⅛ inch, or 3 mm). Then use a small glass, cookie cutter, or a metal measuring cup to cut out small circles.

Lay the dough pieces on the prepared baking sheet. Put 1 teaspoon of pizza sauce on top. Then place 1 pepperoni on top of the sauce. Place another piece of dough on top and pinch the sides together so it closes the pizza pocket. Bake for 17 to 20 minutes, or until the dough is thoroughly cooked on both sides.

As an alternative to the pizza pockets, you can make mini pizzas without adding the top piece of dough.

YIELD: 10 pizza pockets or 20 mini pizzas (without the dough lid)

7

SWEET TREATS
Heavenly Little Snacks without the Guilt

Many times people ask me if I miss cookies and cakes now that I follow a Paleo diet. Fortunately, it is so easy to honestly tell them, "Not at all." I really don't. I just don't have the desire to eat something that will make me feel crummy, especially when it is possible to have so many great-tasting Paleo alternatives.

Some of the Paleo sweet treats out there tend to use dates or other high-glycemic ingredients. While I strive to use sweeteners, such as coconut palm sugar, that have lower glycemic loads, which won't dramatically affect blood sugar levels, it is important to note that some of the treats in this chapter have more calories (than the suggested 200 or so for snacks) and/or more sweetener than the other snacks in this book. With that said, enjoy them, but only on occasion.

The key to successful Paleo treats is in re-creating the texture. The right combination of flours, oils, and particular natural sugars can make a big difference. After years of baking this way, I have discovered some tricks to making these sweet treats taste as close to the original treats we all remember from our youth.

Our taste buds play a big role in how much we like, or don't like, something. If we are used to eating lots of sugar, then a lower-sugar treat, like, say, an apple, might not be quite as satisfying to our palates. The good news is that we can change our taste buds to appreciate more natural foods with less sugar. If you or someone in your family has a particularly strong sweet tooth, feel free to add an extra teaspoon of sweetener here or there (after tasting the batter) to any of the recipes in this book. The treat will still be much healthier than any traditional option out there.

Know that while writing this book, I had my family, neighbors, and friends—especially the self-professed "sugar addicts"—sample all of the recipes for approval. Fortunately, the recipes in this chapter (as well as the others), all eventually passed the test through much trial and error. Now I am excited and proud to share these recipes with you. I hope you like these as much as we do!

MINT CHOCOLATE CHIP BALLS

Reminiscent of Girl Scout Thin Mints, these bite-size little treats will make your taste buds want to sing around the campfire. With a crunchy texture and a minty-sweet taste, this snack will be loved by all. And unlike many Paleo snack balls (or bars) that use high-glycemic sugars, like dates, these will keep your blood sugars stable.

1 cup (145 g) almonds

½ cup (69 g) cashews

½ cup (113 g) pepitas

⅓ cup (115 g) coconut nectar or raw honey

¼ cup (41 g) chia seeds

¼ cup (88 g) dark chocolate chips

3 tablespoons (15 g) raw cacao powder

1 tablespoon (8 g) flaxseed meal

1 tablespoon (15 ml) extra-virgin coconut oil

½ teaspoon peppermint extract

Using a food processor, grind the almonds, cashews, and pepitas together until they are finely chopped. You don't want a flour texture, so don't blend it too much. Then add the coconut nectar, chia seeds, chocolate chips, cacao powder, flaxseed meal, coconut oil, and peppermint extract to the processor and blend until well combined. Remove the mixture from the processor and use your hands to roll the dough into golf ball–size dollops.

Store in an airtight container in the fridge or freezer. Place in a small protective container and take with you in the morning to be enjoyed later at snack time.

YIELD: about 24 balls

BLONDE MACAROONS

Macaroons are always a tasty sweet treat, but add some salt and crunch to this delectable snack and you'll be in heaven. The good news is that since they are made primarily with shredded coconut, the fat will quickly be used for energy, rather than stored in your body. The only thing that will be stored are the leftovers (if there are any!).

6 egg whites

½ teaspoon sea salt

3 cups (240 g) unsweetened shredded coconut

½ cup (170 g) maple syrup or raw honey

1 teaspoon vanilla extract

2 tablespoons (22 g) toasted flaxseeds

2 tablespoons (28 g) roasted and salted sunflower seeds

Preheat the oven to 350°F (180°C, or gas mark 4). Line a baking sheet with parchment paper.

In a mixing bowl with a hand mixer, whisk the egg whites and salt until stiff. Add in the coconut, maple syrup, and vanilla and stir until well combined. Fold in the flaxseeds and sunflower seeds. Using a tablespoon, scoop out the batter and place it onto the prepared baking sheet, about 1 inch (2.5 cm) apart. Bake for 15 minutes, or until lightly brown.

YIELD: 25 to 30 macaroons

MINI PEANUT BUTTER BANANA CUPS

Similar to Reese's Peanut Butter Cups but a heck of a lot healthier and with a fun twist of banana, these little things won't last long in your home. And, even though they are similar to a candy "bar," they are low in sugar and high in antioxidants, so enjoy these guilt-free!

1 cup (175 g) dark chocolate chips

½ cup (130 g) creamy roasted almond butter, peanut butter, or sunflower seed butter

2 tablespoons (40 g) maple syrup

½ teaspoon vanilla extract

1 banana

In a heat-safe bowl, add the chocolate chips and set the bowl over a saucepan of simmering water to melt the chocolate. Before the chocolate is completely melted, remove the bowl from the heat and stir the chocolate until it is smooth. Line 12 cups of a mini-muffin pan with silicone or paper muffin liners and pour about 1 teaspoon of melted chocolate into each cup so it just covers the bottom.

Place the pan in the freezer for about 10 minutes. While that is cooling, in a small bowl, mix together the nut butter, maple syrup, and vanilla. Once the chocolate in the freezer has solidi-fied, add about ¾ teaspoon of nut butter mixture on top of the chocolate, gently shake the pan to get the nut butter to spread out evenly, and then place the pan back in the freezer. While that is cooling, slice a banana into slices that are ¼-inch (6 mm) thick. Once the nut butter has hardened, add a banana slice on top of the nut butter. Then top with more melted chocolate and place the pan back in the freezer for 30 minutes so it can set.

YIELD: 12 cups

VANILLA CUPCAKES WITH CHOCOLATE FROSTING

My daughter, who doesn't care for most baked goods (Paleo or not), absolutely loved these and so did the rest of our family, neighbors, and friends. Words cannot do justice to these, so you'll just have to try them for yourself! No one will ever know they are a much healthier alternative (gluten-free, fiber-filled, and lower-glycemic) to traditional cupcakes.

For the cupcakes:
- 1 cup (192 g) coconut palm sugar
- ½ cup (56 g) coconut flour
- 1 tablespoon (8 g) psyllium husk powder
- ½ teaspoon sea salt
- ¼ teaspoon baking soda
- 6 eggs, at room temperature
- ½ cup (112 g) grass-fed butter, melted
- 1 tablespoon (15 ml) vanilla extract

For the frosting:
- ¾ cup (131 g) dark chocolate chips
- 6 tablespoons (90 ml) unsweetened canned coconut milk (stirred first)
- 1 teaspoon vanilla extract

Preheat the oven to 350°F (180°C, or gas mark 4). Line a 12-cup muffin pan with silicone or paper muffin liners, or grease the cups.

To make the cupcakes: In a medium bowl, combine the coconut palm sugar, coconut flour, psyllium husk powder, salt, and baking soda and mix well. In a separate bowl, whisk the eggs and then beat in the melted butter and vanilla. Once that is mixed together, add it to the dry ingredients and combine.

Pour the batter into the prepared muffin cups about two-thirds full. Bake for 20 minutes or until a toothpick inserted in the middle of a cupcake comes out clean. Allow them to cool completely before topping with frosting.

To make the frosting: In a heat-safe bowl, add the chocolate chips and set the bowl over a saucepan of simmering water, and let the chocolate begin to melt. Then, stir in the milk and vanilla. Just before all of the chocolate is melted, remove the bowl from the heat and stir until smooth. Allow to cool for approximately 5 minutes. Then top the cupcakes with frosting using a butter knife.

YIELD: 12 cupcakes

CINNAMON DONUT HOLES

Since I made the switch to Paleo, I think I miss donuts the most. They are hard to re-create in a Paleo form because of the texture. Needless to say, I was so excited the first time I made these because they tasted like, and had the texture of, a real donut! These absolutely amazing, nut-free, fiber-filled, low-sugar, heavenly mouthwatering treats will make you think the "HOT" sign (from Krispy Kreme) is back on!

½ cup (56 g) coconut flour

2 tablespoons (16 g) psyllium husk powder

¼ cup (48 g) coconut palm sugar, plus 2 tablespoons (24 g) for dipping

¼ teaspoon sea salt

1 cup (235 ml) water

¼ cup (55 g) grass-fed butter, plus 2 tablespoons (28 g) for dipping (can omit to make dairy-free)

1 tablespoon (7 g) cinnamon

Preheat the oven 325°F (170°C, or gas mark 3). Line a baking sheet with parchment paper.

In a medium bowl, mix together the coconut flour, psyllium husk powder, ¼ cup (48 g) coconut palm sugar, and salt. In a small pot, boil the water, turn off the heat, and then add ¼ cup (55 g) butter and stir until the butter is melted. Add the wet ingredients to the dry. When the mixture has cooled enough for you to handle, squish the dough together until it forms a firm ball.

Tear off golf ball–size pieces of dough and form them into donut holes. Place the balls on the prepared baking sheet. Melt the remaining 2 tablespoons butter in a small bowl. In another small bowl, mix together the remaining 2 tablespoons coconut palm sugar and the cinnamon. Take each donut hole dough ball and dip it in the butter, making sure to coat it all over. Then, roll it into the sugar-cinnamon mixture. Place it back on the baking sheet and repeat until you have covered all of the balls of dough. Bake for about 25 minutes or until a toothpick inserted in the middle comes out clean. Eat them while they are warm!

Alternatively (or in addition to), if you don't want to use cinnamon, you could melt some dark chocolate and drizzle it over the donut holes once they come out of the oven. Mmmmm.

YIELD: about 12 donut holes

"CHEESECAKE" BITES WITH CARAMEL SAUCE

Cheesecake without cheese? Yep! And you won't miss the dairy, filled with casein or lactose that can be so irritating to the gut. This rich and creamy caramel dessert will make you wonder why everyone doesn't always choose a healthy alternative.

For the cheesecake bites:

1½ cups (390 g) raw cashew butter

½ cup (170 g) maple syrup

3 tablespoons (45 ml) lemon juice

1 teaspoon vanilla extract

¼ teaspoon sea salt

For the caramel sauce:

¾ cup (175 ml) unsweetened canned coconut milk (stirred first)

¾ cup (144 g) coconut palm sugar

¼ cup (55 g) grass-fed butter

2 teaspoons (10 ml) vanilla extract

To make the cheesecake bites: In a large bowl, mix together the cashew butter, maple syrup, lemon juice, vanilla, and salt. Pour into a 7 × 7-inch (18 × 18 cm) glass dish and put it in the freezer. While that is cooling, make the caramel topping.

To make the caramel sauce: In a small saucepan over medium heat, stir the coconut milk and palm sugar together until well blended. Bring to a boil and then reduce it to a simmer. Add the butter and continue stirring for about 10 minutes, or until it thickens. Take it off the stove and let it cool for a few minutes. Then stir in the vanilla. Allow to cool for about 20 minutes while the cheesecake is still cooling in the freezer.

Once everything has had a chance to cool, pour the sauce over the cheesecake and freeze overnight. When you are ready to serve, cut out your bite-size squares with a pizza cutter and serve immediately. Be sure to serve frozen for an authentic cheesecake texture.

The caramel topping is also great on almost any sweet treat. Or try it on fruit!

YIELD: about 12 bites

HAPPY BIRTHDAY COOKIE CAKE

Crispy cookie cake that is Paleo!? Impossible, you say? Not with this recipe. Fresh out of the oven, the outside is crispy, and the ooey-gooey middle will remind you of a traditional cookie cake. The birthday girl or boy will never know it's Paleo!

- 2 cups (520 g) almond or cashew butter
- 4 eggs
- 1 cup (340 g) maple syrup
- ½ cup (112 g) grass-fed butter, melted
- 2 tablespoons (16 g) arrowroot powder
- 2 teaspoons (10 ml) vanilla extract
- 1 teaspoon baking soda
- ½ teaspoon sea salt
- 1 cup (175 g) plus 1 cup (175 g) (optional) dark chocolate chips, divided

Preheat the oven to 325°F (170°C, or gas mark 3). Grease an 8 x 13-inch (20 x 33 cm) baking dish or a 9-inch (23 cm) pie plate.

In a medium bowl, combine the almond butter, eggs, maple syrup, butter, arrowroot powder, vanilla, baking soda, and salt with a hand mixer or fork. Then fold in 1 cup (175 g) of the chocolate chips. Pour the batter into the prepared pan, and bake for 35 to 50 minutes. If you want it a little gooey in the middle, cook it for 35. If you want it a little more firm and crispy, cook it for about 50 minutes, or until a toothpick inserted in the middle comes out clean.

To add the optional chocolate topping, in a medium heat-safe bowl, add the remaining 1 cup (175 g) chocolate chips and set the bowl over a saucepan of simmering water. Let the chocolate melt. Before the chocolate is completely melted, remove the bowl from the heat and stir the chocolate until it is smooth. Spread over the cake, let cool for about 10 minutes, and enjoy.

YIELD: 8 to 12 servings

MINTY THINS

Year after year, the Girl Scouts' Thin Mint cookies bring in the most sales. And it's no wonder why, with their crispy texture and sweet minty flavor. Unfortunately, with hydrogenated oil and unhealthy preservatives, Thin Mints are a cookie I can live without. Fortunately, with this recipe, we don't have to miss them. These are so good, it's hard to tell them apart from the originals, except you'll feel much better after eating these.

½ cup (112 g) plus 3 tablespoons (45 g) grass-fed butter, melted and divided

¼ cup (85 g) maple syrup

¼ cup (20 g) raw cacao powder

1 teaspoon baking soda

1 teaspoon peppermint extract

1 egg

¾ cup (84 g) coconut flour

1½ cups (263 g) dark chocolate chips

In a medium bowl, blend together ½ cup (112 g) of the butter, maple syrup, cacao powder, baking soda, and peppermint extract with a hand mixer or a whisk. In a small bowl, beat the egg and then add it to the butter-syrup mixture. Mix well until it forms a soft batter. Mix in the coconut flour in small increments until well combined. On parchment paper, hand roll the dough into a long cylinder (2½ to 3 inches, or 6.5 to 7.5 cm, thick) and refrigerate for 30 minutes.

Preheat the oven to 350°F (180°C, or gas mark 4). Once the dough has hardened, slice the dough into ¼-inch (6 mm) rounds and place them onto a baking sheet lined with parchment paper. Bake for 7 to 9 minutes, or until set, and then allow to cool for 30 minutes.

In a heat-safe bowl, add the chocolate chips and remaining 3 tablespoons (45 g) butter and set the bowl over a saucepan of simmering water to let the chocolate and butter melt. Before the chocolate is completely melted, remove the bowl from the heat and stir the chocolate until it is smooth. Allow the chocolate to cool for about 10 minutes. Once it is cool, dip each cookie and cover it completely with chocolate (it will get a little messy) and then place the cookie on the parchment paper. Once you finish coating all the cookies, place the baking sheet in the fridge so they can cool and harden. Store them in a sealed container in the fridge or freezer.

YIELD: 36 cookies

N'OATMEAL COOKIES

When I was a young child, my grandma used to make oatmeal raisin cookies made with Crisco, white flour, sugar, and oats. I remember going back again and again to her metal tin for just one more cookie. And while these are, from a health standpoint, the antithesis of her old-fashioned cookies, they are equally as good. Grandma would have approved!

- 2 cups (200 g) almond meal
- ½ cup (96 g) coconut palm sugar
- 2 tablespoons (16 g) arrowroot powder
- 1 tablespoon (7 g) cinnamon
- 1 teaspoon sea salt
- ¾ teaspoon baking soda
- 4 eggs, at room temperature
- ½ cup (112 g) grass-fed butter, melted
- ¼ cup (85 g) maple syrup
- 1 teaspoon vanilla extract
- ½ cup (50 g) raw walnuts, roughly chopped
- ½ cup (50 g) raw pecans, roughly chopped
- ½ cup (73 g) raw almonds, roughly chopped
- ½ cup (75 g) raisins

Preheat the oven to 350°F (180°C, or gas mark 4). Line a baking sheet with parchment paper.

In a small bowl, mix together the almond meal, coconut palm sugar, arrowroot, cinnamon, salt, and baking soda. In a medium bowl, beat the eggs, and then mix in the butter, maple syrup, and vanilla. Pour the dry ingredients into the wet and combine well. Then fold in the walnuts, pecans, almonds, and raisins.

Use your hands or a tablespoon to shape the dough into 2½-inch (6.5 cm) cookies. Bake for 8 to 10 minutes, or until set.

YIELD: about 18 cookies

MOLTEN LAVA CAKES

Words can't even begin to describe this mouthwatering treat. Warm, gooey, sweet, chocolaty goodness. Yes, please! What more could anyone want? And they're simple to make: My nine-year-old makes this completely by herself on the weekends for a fun family treat! To make this nut-free, use 1½ teaspoons coconut flour instead of the almond flour.

¾ cup (131 g) dark chocolate chips or chopped bar chocolate

½ cup (112 g) grass-fed butter

⅓ cup (115 g) maple syrup

1 tablespoon (5 g) raw cacao powder

½ teaspoon vanilla extract

2 eggs

2 egg yolks

2 tablespoons (14 g) almond flour

¼ teaspoon salt

Preheat the oven to 400°F (200°C, or gas mark 6). Grease four 6-ounce (170 g) ramekins or 8 cups in a muffin pan if you don't have ramekins.

In a small saucepan over low heat, melt the chocolate and butter. As the chocolate is melting, stir in the maple syrup, cacao powder, and vanilla and remove the saucepan from the burner.

In a medium bowl, beat or whisk the eggs and yolks. Slowly add the chocolate mixture to the eggs while continuously whisking. Add in the almond flour and salt and stir well. Divide the batter among the prepared ramekins. Place on a baking sheet and bake for 10 minutes, or until a toothpick inserted in the side of a cake comes out clean. (The centers should still be soft and gooey.) Eat straight out of cup holders or flip upside side onto a serving plate and serve immediately.

YIELD: 4 large or 8 small cakes

APPLE CRUMBLE

This has the all-American appeal of apple pie, but without loads of sugar and gluten. And even better, it's so much easier to prepare sans the pie crust. These warm baked apples with a light sweetness make for the perfect fall treat!

7 small or 5 medium apples, peeled, cored, and quartered

2 cups (224 g) blanched almond flour

¼ cup (48 g) coconut palm sugar

1 teaspoon cinnamon

½ teaspoon nutmeg

½ teaspoon sea salt

⅓ cup (75 g) grass-fed butter, melted

3 tablespoons (60 g) raw honey

1 tablespoon (15 ml) vanilla extract

¼ cup (25 g) walnuts, finely chopped (optional)

Preheat the oven to 350°F (180°C, or gas mark 4). Place the apples in an 8 x 8-inch (20 x 20 cm) or a 7 x 11-inch (18 x 28 cm) baking dish and spread them out evenly.

In a large bowl, combine the almond flour, coconut palm sugar, cinnamon, nutmeg, and salt. In a small bowl, combine the butter, honey, and vanilla. Stir the wet ingredients into the dry and then crumble the topping over the apples. Cover with foil and bake on a low rack for 50 to 60 minutes, or until the apples are soft and their juices bubble. Remove the foil and bake for 10 more minutes to brown the top. Then add the walnuts, if using, to the top.

YIELD: 8 servings

CHOCOLATE-COVERED COOKIES

To tell you the truth, the first time we made "Paleo" chocolate chip cookies, they were, well, just okay. After years of experimenting with Paleo flours and ingredients, I've finally found a Paleo cookie that is pretty close to perfect— cakey, buttery, crispy around the edges, delicious.

1⅓ cups (150 g) almond flour

1 cup (192 g) coconut palm sugar

2 tablespoons (14 g) coconut flour

2 tablespoons (16 g) arrowroot powder

1 teaspoon baking soda

½ teaspoon sea salt

3 eggs

½ cup (112 g) grass-fed butter, melted

2 teaspoons (10 ml) vanilla extract

1 cup (175 g) dark chocolate chips

Preheat the oven to 350°F (180°C, or gas mark 4). Line a baking sheet with parchment paper.

In a medium bowl, mix together the almond flour, coconut palm sugar, coconut flour, arrowroot, baking soda, and salt. In a small bowl, beat the eggs, and then add in the melted butter and vanilla. Pour the egg mixture into the dry ingredients and mix until smooth. If you prefer, you can fold in the chocolate chips here, or see below for directions on melting the chocolate for covering the cookies.

Place tablespoon-size balls of batter 1 to 2 inches (2.5 to 5 cm) apart on the prepared baking sheet. Flatten them a little so they will be shaped like a cookie. Bake for 8 to 10 minutes, or until set. Set aside to cool while you make the chocolate coating.

In a heat-safe bowl, add the chocolate chips and set the bowl over a saucepan of simmering water, and let the chocolate melt. Before the chocolate is completely melted, remove the bowl from the heat and stir the chocolate until it is smooth. Dip each cookie facedown and return to a metal rack or plate to cool completely.

YIELD: about 24 cookies

SNICKERDOODLE COOKIE DOUGH BITES

The only thing better than a snickerdoodle is snickerdoodle batter. When I used to make these the traditional way, I would eat the batter with my fingers crossed, hoping that the raw egg wouldn't make me sick. No worries with this recipe. It is a completely safe and a much healthier way, sans the gluten and processed sugar, to eat batter.

1 cup (112 g) almond flour

¾ cup (144 g) plus 4 teaspoons (16 g) coconut palm sugar, divided

½ cup (130 g) almond butter

½ cup (112 g) grass-fed butter, melted

¼ cup (28 g) coconut flour

1 teaspoon vanilla extract

¼ teaspoon sea salt

Handful of dark chocolate chips (optional)

1½ teaspoons (3.5 g) cinnamon

In a bowl, mix together the almond flour, ¾ cup (144 g) coconut palm sugar, almond butter, butter, coconut flour, vanilla, and salt. If using chocolate chips, add them now. With your hands, form into golf ball–size balls.

In a small bowl, mix together the remaining 4 teaspoons (16 g) coconut palm sugar and the cinnamon. Roll the balls into the mixture until they're completely covered.

Store in an airtight container in the fridge for up to 2 weeks.

YIELD: 20 to 24 bites

INDEX

A

almond butter
Banana-Blueberry Power Squares, 130
Blonde Snack Bars, 60
Cherry-Cacao Energy Balls, 131
Chocolate Banana Smoothie, 141
Chocolate Chip Muffins, 123
Cinnamon Raisin Bars, 124
Happy Birthday Cookie Cake, 177
Honey Almond Nut Butter, 133
introduction to, 21
Mini Peanut Butter Banana Cups, 170
Pumpkin Bars, 105
Raw Coconut Almond Bonbons, 119
Snickerdoodle Cookie Dough Bites, 185
Supersmart Bars, 63
Sweet Potato Power Brownies, 128
almond flour
Almond Cheese Crackers, 106
Apple Crumble, 183
Banana Walnut Muffins, 142
Buttered Saltine Crackers, 108
Chocolate Chip Muffins, 123
Chocolate-Covered Cookies, 184
Chocolate Muffins, 145
Cinnamon Bun Biscuits, 122
Cinnamon Graham Crackers, 100
Easy-Bake Cake Cup, 96
Flatcake Sandwich Bread, 115
introduction to, 20
Italian Meatballs, 56
Mediterranean Bread, 49
Mini Zucchini Muffins, 125
Molten Lava Cakes, 182
My Favorite Crunchy Crackers, 114
Pancake-Wrapped Sausage, 93
Pigs in a Blanket, 40
Pinwheel Sandwich Bread, 117
Snickerdoodle Cookie Dough Bites, 185
Soft Paleo Pretzels, 88–89
Sweet Potato Casserole Bread, 143
Sweet Potato Pancakes, 147
Sweet Potato Power Brownies, 128
Teriyaki Salmon Cakes, 53
almond meal
Chicken Maple Sausage Meatballs, 48
introduction to, 20
Italian Meatballs, 56
N'Oatmeal Cookies, 180
Onion Rings, 83
Savory Baked Chicken Nuggets, 36
Teriyaki Salmon Cakes, 53
almond milk
Chia Pudding, 146
Chocolate Banana Smoothie, 141
Cinnamon Bun Biscuits, 122

Energizing Chocolate Milk, 97
Green Lemonade Smoothie, 95
Hot Chocolate, 97
introduction to, 28
Onion Rings, 83
Powerhouse Paleo Coffee, 135
almonds
Apple Crumb Bites, 59
Banana Nut Bites, 134
Cherry-Cacao Energy Balls, 131
Chia Pudding, 146
Chocolate Almond Squares, 102
Chocolate Chip Granola Squares, 103
Crispy Maple Granola, 112
Crunchy Granola Brittle, 132
Honey Almond Nut Butter, 133
Kale Salad, 72
Mint Chocolate Chip Balls, 168
Ranch "Cheese" Ball, 90
Raw Coconut Almond Bonbons, 119
American Academy of Pediatrics, 19
apples
Apple Crisp Chips, 109
Apple Crumb Bites, 59
Apple Crumble, 183
Apple Pie Trail Mix Balls, 152
Green Lemonade Smoothie, 95
arrowroot powder, introduction to, 21
artichoke hearts
Artichoke Pesto, 92
Egg Muffins, 51
Mediterranean Bread, 49
asparagus. See Prosciutto-Wrapped
Asparagus, 81
avocados
Creamy Zucchini, 77
Green Deviled Eggs & Bacon, 71

B

bacon
Bacon Cauliflower Soup, 42
Bacon & Egg Maple Muffins, 39
Bacon & Sweet Potato Hash, 144
Green Deviled Eggs & Bacon, 71
Ranch "Cheese" Ball, 90
Sweet Bacon Kale, 87
baking soda, introduction to, 29
bananas
Banana-Blueberry Power Squares, 130
Banana Nut Bites, 134
Banana Walnut Muffins, 142
Chocolate Banana Smoothie, 141
Green Lemonade Smoothie, 95
Mini Peanut Butter Banana Cups, 170
Powerhouse Paleo Coffee, 135
Silver Dollar Banana Pancakes, 111

beef
Homemade Beef Jerky, 43
Italian Meatballs, 56
Mexican Muffins, 52
Best Nut-Free Muffins Around, 156
Bhatia, Tasneem, 8–9
blenders, 32
Blonde Macaroons, 169
Blonde Snack Bars, 60
blueberries
Banana-Blueberry Power Squares, 130
Blueberry Muffins, 65
Chia Pudding, 146
Cinnamon Blueberry Bread, 64
Pumpkin-Spiced Granola Bars, 150
Superfruity Roll-Ups, 116
Brussels sprouts
Kale Salad, 72
Zesty Walnut Brussels Sprouts, 84
Buffalo Chicken Wings, 55
butter, introduction to, 27
Butternut Squash Fritters, 78

C

cacao powder, introduction to, 24
carob, introduction to, 24
cashew butter
"Cheesecake" Bites with Caramel Sauce, 176
Happy Birthday Cookie Cake, 177
introduction to, 21–22
cashew flour
Easy "Cheese" Kale Chips, 76
Savory Baked Chicken Nuggets, 36
Sweet Potato Pancakes, 147
cashews
"Cheesecake" Bites with Caramel Sauce, 176
Chocolate Chip Granola Squares, 103
Crunchy Granola Brittle, 132
Easy "Cheese" Kale Chips, 76
Happy Birthday Cookie Cake, 177
Mint Chocolate Chip Balls, 168
Ranch "Cheese" Ball, 90
Supersmart Bars, 63
cauliflower
Bacon Cauliflower Soup, 42
Cauliflower Hummus, 75
Cauliflower Pizza Bites, 47
Cheddar cheese
Almond Cheese Crackers, 106
Egg Muffins, 51
Mexican Muffins, 52
"Cheesecake" Bites with Caramel Sauce, 176
cherries
Cherry-Cacao Energy Balls, 131
Pumpkin-Spiced Granola Bars, 150

chia seeds
    Chia Pudding, 146
    Chocolate Chia Workout Bars, 137
    Chocolate Chip Granola Squares, 103
    Crispy Four-Seed Granola, 159
    Crispy Maple Granola, 112
    Crunchy Granola Brittle, 132
    Crunchy Omega-3 Flax Granola, 153
    introduction to, 23
    Mint Chocolate Chip Balls, 168
    My Favorite Crunchy Crackers, 114
    Powerhouse Paleo Coffee, 135
    Pumpkin-Spiced Granola Bars, 150
chicken
    Buffalo Chicken Wings, 55
    Chicken Maple Sausage Meatballs, 48
    Savory Baked Chicken Nuggets, 36
    Sun-Dried Tomato Chicken Sliders, 44
chocolate
    Best Nut-Free Muffins Around, 156
    Blonde Snack Bars, 60
    Cherry-Cacao Energy Balls, 131
    Chia Pudding, 146
    Chocolate Almond Squares, 102
    Chocolate Banana Smoothie, 141
    Chocolate Chia Workout Bars, 137
    Chocolate Chip Granola Squares, 103
    Chocolate Chip Muffins, 123
    Chocolate-Covered Cookies, 184
    Chocolate Muffins, 145
    Chocolate Sunflower Seed Butter, 157
    Chocolate Zucchini "Bread," 164
    Easy-Bake Cake Cup, 96
    Energizing Chocolate Milk, 97
    Happy Birthday Cookie Cake, 177
    Hot Chocolate, 97
    introduction to, 23–24
    Mini Peanut Butter Banana Cups, 170
    Mint Chocolate Chip Balls, 168
    Minty Thins, 179
    Molten Lava Cakes, 182
    "Peanut Butter" Patties, 155
    Powerhouse Paleo Coffee, 135
    Pumpkin Chocolate Chip Muffins, 61
    Raw Coconut Almond Bonbons, 119
    Snickerdoodle Cookie Dough Bites, 185
    Supersmart Bars, 63
    Sweet Potato Power Brownies, 128
    Vanilla Cupcakes with Chocolate Frosting, 173
Cinnamon Blueberry Bread, 64
Cinnamon Bun Biscuits, 122
Cinnamon Donut Holes, 174
Cinnamon Graham Crackers, 100
Cinnamon Raisin Bars, 124
coconut
    Apple Crumb Bites, 59

Apple Pie Trail Mix Balls, 152
Blonde Macaroons, 169
Chocolate Almond Squares, 102
Chocolate Chia Workout Bars, 137
Chocolate Chip Granola Squares, 103
Crispy Four-Seed Granola, 159
Crispy Maple Granola, 112
Crunchy Omega-3 Flax Granola, 153
introduction to, 31
Onion Rings, 83
Pancake-Wrapped Sausage, 93
Pumpkin-Spiced Granola Bars, 150
Raw Coconut Almond Bonbons, 119
Supersmart Bars, 63
coconut aminos
    Homemade Beef Jerky, 43
    Teriyaki Salmon Cakes, 53
coconut butter
    Chocolate Chia Workout Bars, 137
    Chocolate Sunflower Seed Butter, 157
    Cinnamon Bun Biscuits, 122
    introduction to, 21
coconut flour
    Bacon & Egg Maple Muffins, 39
    Banana-Blueberry Power Squares, 130
    Banana Walnut Muffins, 142
    Blueberry Muffins, 65
    Buttered Saltine Crackers, 108
    Chicken Maple Sausage Meatballs, 48
    Chocolate-Covered Cookies, 184
    Chocolate Muffins, 145
    Cinnamon Blueberry Bread, 64
    Cinnamon Donut Holes, 174
    Easy-Bake Cake Cup, 96
    Flatbread "PB&J," 158
    Flatcake Sandwich Bread, 115
    introduction to, 20
    Minty Thins, 179
    "Peanut Butter" Patties, 155
    Pizza Pockets, 165
    Pumpkin Bars, 105
    Pumpkin Chocolate Chip Muffins, 61
    Snickerdoodle Cookie Dough Bites, 185
    Soft Paleo Pretzels, 88–89
    Sweet Potato Casserole Bread, 143
    Vanilla Cupcakes with Chocolate Frosting, 173
coconut milk
    Bacon Cauliflower Soup, 42
    Bacon & Egg Maple Muffins, 39
    Banana-Blueberry Power Squares, 130
    "Cheesecake" Bites with Caramel Sauce, 176
    Chia Pudding, 146
    Chocolate Banana Smoothie, 141
    Cinnamon Blueberry Bread, 64
    Cinnamon Bun Biscuits, 122
    Flatcake Sandwich Bread, 115

introduction to, 28
Mediterranean Bread, 49
Onion Rings, 83
Pancake-Wrapped Sausage, 93
Pigs in a Blanket, 40
Pinwheel Sandwich Bread, 117
Pumpkin Chocolate Chip Muffins, 61
Vanilla Cupcakes with Chocolate Frosting, 173
coconut nectar
    Apple Pie Trail Mix Balls, 152
    Chocolate Almond Squares, 102
    introduction to, 25
    Mint Chocolate Chip Balls, 168
    Pumpkin-Spiced Granola Bars, 150
    Raw Coconut Almond Bonbons, 119
    Supersmart Bars, 63
coconut oil, introduction to, 27
coconut palm sugar
    Apple Crisp Chips, 109
    Apple Crumb Bites, 59
    Apple Crumble, 183
    Apple Pie Trail Mix Balls, 152
    Banana Walnut Muffins, 142
    Best Nut-Free Muffins Around, 156
    Blonde Snack Bars, 60
    Blueberry Muffins, 65
    "Cheesecake" Bites with Caramel Sauce, 176
    Cherry-Cacao Energy Balls, 131
    Chocolate Almond Squares, 102
    Chocolate Chip Muffins, 123
    Chocolate-Covered Cookies, 184
    Cinnamon Bun Biscuits, 122
    Cinnamon Donut Holes, 174
    Cinnamon Raisin Bars, 124
    Crispy Four-Seed Granola, 159
    Crunchy Omega-3 Flax Granola, 153
    Easy-Bake Cake Cup, 96
    Energizing Chocolate Milk, 97
    Hot Chocolate, 97
    introduction to, 25
    Mini Zucchini Muffins, 125
    N'Oatmeal Cookies, 180
    "Peanut Butter" Cookies, 163
    Pumpkin Bars, 105
    Pumpkin Chocolate Chip Muffins, 61
    Raw Coconut Almond Bonbons, 119
    Silver Dollar Banana Pancakes, 111
    Snickerdoodle Cookie Dough Bites, 185
    Sweet Potato Casserole Bread, 143
    Sweet Potato Power Brownies, 128
    Vanilla Cupcakes with Chocolate Frosting, 173
coconut water
    Green Lemonade Smoothie, 95
    Powerhouse Paleo Coffee, 135
cranberries. See Kale Salad, 72
Creamy Zucchini, 77

Crispy Four-Seed Granola, 159
Crispy Maple Granola, 112
Crispy Okra Sticks, 68
Crunchy Granola Brittle, 132
Crunchy Omega-3 Flax Granola, 153
Crunchy Sweet Potato Fries, 138
currants
    Cinnamon Raisin Bars, 124
    Mini Zucchini Muffins, 125

D
dairy-free snacks
    Apple Crisp Chips, 109
    Apple Pie Trail Mix Balls, 152
    Artichoke Pesto, 92
    Bacon Cauliflower Soup, 42
    Bacon & Sweet Potato Hash, 144
    Banana-Blueberry Power Squares, 130
    Blonde Snack Bars, 60
    Blueberry Muffins, 65
    Buffalo Chicken Wings, 55
    Cauliflower Hummus, 75
    Cherry-Cacao Energy Balls, 131
    Chia Pudding, 146
    Chicken Maple Sausage Meatballs, 48
    Chocolate Almond Squares, 102
    Chocolate Banana Smoothie, 141
    Chocolate Chia Workout Bars, 137
    Chocolate Chip Granola Squares, 103
    Chocolate Chip Muffins, 123
    Chocolate Muffins, 145
    Chocolate Sunflower Seed Butter, 157
    Chocolate Zucchini "Bread," 164
    Cinnamon Graham Crackers, 100
    Creamy Zucchini, 77
    Crispy Four-Seed Granola, 159
    Crispy Okra Sticks, 68
    Crunchy Granola Brittle, 132
    Crunchy Omega-3 Flax Granola, 153
    Crunchy Sweet Potato Fries, 138
    Easy-Bake Cake Cup, 96
    Easy "Cheese" Kale Chips, 76
    Energizing Chocolate Milk, 97
    Flatbread "PB&J," 158
    Flatcake Sandwich Bread, 115
    Green Deviled Eggs & Bacon, 71
    Green Lemonade Smoothie, 95
    Homemade Beef Jerky, 43
    Honey Almond Nut Butter, 133
    Hot Chocolate, 97
    introduction to, 33
    Italian Meatballs, 56
    Mini Peanut Butter Banana Cups, 170
    Mint Chocolate Chip Balls, 168
    My Favorite Crunchy Crackers, 114
    Onion Rings, 83
    Pancake-Wrapped Sausage, 93
    Powerhouse Paleo Coffee, 135
    Prosciutto-Wrapped Asparagus, 81
    Pumpkin Bars, 105
    Pumpkin Chocolate Chip Muffins, 61
    Pumpkin-Spiced Granola Bars, 150
    Ranch "Cheese" Ball, 90
    Raw Coconut Almond Bonbons, 119
    Roasted Red Pepper Dip, 91
    Squash Chips, 82
    Strawberry Gummies, 120
    Sun-Dried Tomato Chicken Sliders, 44
    Superfruity Roll-Ups, 116
    Supersmart Bars, 63
    Sweet Bacon Kale, 87

Sweet Potato Casserole Bread, 143
Sweet Potato Pancakes, 147
Sweet & Salty Spiced Pepitas, 160
Teriyaki Salmon Cakes, 53
Zesty Walnut Brussels Sprouts, 84

E
Easy-Bake Cake Cup, 96
Easy "Cheese" Kale Chips, 76
egg-free snacks
    Apple Crisp Chips, 109
    Apple Crumble, 183
    Apple Pie Trail Mix Balls, 152
    Artichoke Pesto, 92
    Bacon Cauliflower Soup, 42
    Bacon & Sweet Potato Hash, 144
    Banana Nut Bites, 134
    Cauliflower Hummus, 75
    "Cheesecake" Bites with Caramel Sauce, 176
    Cherry-Cacao Energy Balls, 131
    Chia Pudding, 146
    Chocolate Almond Squares, 102
    Chocolate Banana Smoothie, 141
    Chocolate Chia Workout Bars, 137
    Chocolate Chip Granola Squares, 103
    Chocolate Sunflower Seed Butter, 157
    Cinnamon Donut Holes, 174
    Cinnamon Graham Crackers, 100
    Creamy Zucchini, 77
    Crispy Four-Seed Granola, 159
    Crispy Maple Granola, 112
    Crispy Okra Sticks, 68
    Crunchy Granola Brittle, 132
    Crunchy Omega-3 Flax Granola, 153
    Crunchy Sweet Potato Fries, 138
    Easy "Cheese" Kale Chips, 76
    Energizing Chocolate Milk, 97
    Flatbread "PB&J," 158
    Green Lemonade Smoothie, 95
    Homemade Beef Jerky, 43
    Honey Almond Nut Butter, 133
    Hot Chocolate, 97
    introduction to, 33
    Kale Salad, 72
    Mini Peanut Butter Banana Cups, 170
    Mint Chocolate Chip Balls, 168
    Pigs in a Blanket, 40
    Pinwheel Sandwich Bread, 117
    Pizza Pockets, 165
    Powerhouse Paleo Coffee, 135
    Prosciutto-Wrapped Asparagus, 81
    Pumpkin-Spiced Granola Bars, 150
    Ranch "Cheese" Ball, 90
    Raw Coconut Almond Bonbons, 119
    Roasted Red Pepper Dip, 91
    Savory Baked Chicken Nuggets, 36
    Snickerdoodle Cookie Dough Bites, 185
    Squash Chips, 82
    Strawberry Gummies, 120
    Sun-Dried Tomato Chicken Sliders, 44
    Superfruity Roll-Ups, 116
    Supersmart Bars, 63
    Sweet Bacon Kale, 87
    Sweet & Salty Spiced Pepitas, 160
    Zesty Walnut Brussels Sprouts, 84
eggs
    Apple Crumb Bites, 59
    Bacon & Egg Maple Muffins, 39
    Banana-Blueberry Power Squares, 130
    Banana Walnut Muffins, 142
    Best Nut-Free Muffins Around, 156

Blonde Macaroons, 169
Blonde Snack Bars, 60
Blueberry Muffins, 65
Buttered Saltine Crackers, 108
Butternut Squash Fritters, 78
Cauliflower Pizza Bites, 47
Chicken Maple Sausage Meatballs, 48
Chocolate Chip Muffins, 123
Chocolate-Covered Cookies, 184
Chocolate Muffins, 145
Chocolate Zucchini "Bread," 164
Cinnamon Blueberry Bread, 64
Cinnamon Bun Biscuits, 122
Cinnamon Raisin Bars, 124
Easy-Bake Cake Cup, 96
Egg Muffins, 51
Flatcake Sandwich Bread, 115
Green Deviled Eggs & Bacon, 71
Happy Birthday Cookie Cake, 177
introduction to, 29
Italian Meatballs, 56
Mediterranean Bread, 49
Mexican Muffins, 52
Mini Zucchini Muffins, 125
Minty Thins, 179
Molten Lava Cakes, 182
My Favorite Crunchy Crackers, 114
Onion Rings, 83
"Peanut Butter" Patties, 155
Pumpkin Bars, 105
Pumpkin Chocolate Chip Muffins, 61
Silver Dollar Banana Pancakes, 111
Soft Paleo Pretzels, 88–89
Sweet Potato Casserole Bread, 143
Sweet Potato Pancakes, 147
Sweet Potato Power Brownies, 128
types of, 30
Vanilla Cupcakes with Chocolate Frosting, 173
Energizing Chocolate Milk, 97

F
Flatbread "PB&J," 158
Flatcake Sandwich Bread, 115
flaxseed meal
    Cinnamon Blueberry Bread, 64
    introduction to, 22–23
    Mediterranean Bread, 49
    Mini Zucchini Muffins, 125
    My Favorite Crunchy Crackers, 114
    Raw Coconut Almond Bonbons, 119
flaxseeds
    Blonde Macaroons, 169
    Chocolate Chip Granola Squares, 103
    Crispy Four-Seed Granola, 159
    Crunchy Granola Brittle, 132
    Crunchy Omega-3 Flax Granola, 153
    introduction to, 22–23
    Pumpkin-Spiced Granola Bars, 150
Food Commission (United Kingdom), 98
food processors, 32

G
gelatin
    introduction to, 31
    Strawberry Gummies, 120
ghee, introduction to, 27–28
goat cheese. See Cauliflower Pizza Bites, 47
Grain Brain (David Perlmutter), 39
grain, 12, 15
Green Deviled Eggs & Bacon, 71
Green Lemonade Smoothie, 95

H

ham. See Egg Muffins, 51
Happy Birthday Cookie Cake, 177
Homemade Beef Jerky, 43
honey
    Apple Crumble, 183
    Banana-Blueberry Power Squares, 130
    Banana Nut Bites, 134
    Blonde Macaroons, 169
    Cherry-Cacao Energy Balls, 131
    Chia Pudding, 146
    Chocolate Chia Workout Bars, 137
    Chocolate Chip Granola Squares, 103
    Chocolate Muffins, 145
    Crunchy Granola Brittle, 132
    Homemade Beef Jerky, 43
    Honey Almond Nut Butter, 133
    introduction to, 25
    Mint Chocolate Chip Balls, 168
    "Peanut Butter" Patties, 155
    Powerhouse Paleo Coffee, 135
    Pumpkin-Spiced Granola Bars, 150
    Strawberry Gummies, 120
    Superfruity Roll-Ups, 116
    Sweet Potato Casserole Bread, 143
    Sweet Potato Pancakes, 147
    Sweet Potato Power Brownies, 128
Hot Chocolate, 97
hot dogs. See Pigs in a Blanket, 40

I

immersion blenders, 32
Italian Meatballs, 56

J

Journal of Nutrition, 14

K

kale
    Easy "Cheese" Kale Chips, 76
    Green Lemonade Smoothie, 95
    Kale Salad, 72
    Sweet Bacon Kale, 87

M

macadamia nuts. See Ranch "Cheese" Ball, 90
mandolin slicers, 32
maple syrup
    Bacon & Egg Maple Muffins, 39
    Bacon & Sweet Potato Hash, 144
    Blonde Macaroons, 169
    Blueberry Muffins, 65
    "Cheesecake" Bites with Caramel Sauce, 176
    Chicken Maple Sausage Meatballs, 48
    Chocolate Sunflower Seed Butter, 157
    Chocolate Zucchini "Bread," 164
    Cinnamon Blueberry Bread, 64
    Cinnamon Bun Biscuits, 122
    Cinnamon Graham Crackers, 100
    Cinnamon Raisin Bars, 124
    Crispy Maple Granola, 112
    Flatcake Sandwich Bread, 115
    Happy Birthday Cookie Cake, 177
    introduction to, 25–26
    Mini Peanut Butter Banana Cups, 170
    Minty Thins, 179
    Molten Lava Cakes, 182
    N'Oatmeal Cookies, 180
    Pancake-Wrapped Sausage, 93
    Pumpkin Bars, 105
    Pumpkin Chocolate Chip Muffins, 61

Silver Dollar Banana Pancakes, 111
    Sweet Potato Pancakes, 147
    Sweet & Salty Spiced Pepitas, 160
Mediterranean Bread, 49
Mexican Muffins, 52
Mini Peanut Butter Banana Cups, 170
Mini Zucchini Muffins, 125
Mint Chocolate Chip Balls, 168
Minty Thins, 179
Molten Lava Cakes, 182
mozzarella cheese. See Cauliflower Pizza
    Bites, 47
mushrooms. See Egg Muffins, 51
My Favorite Crunchy Crackers, 114

N

N'Oatmeal Cookies, 180
nut-free snacks
    Apple Crisp Chips, 109
    Apple Pie Trail Mix Balls, 152
    Bacon Cauliflower Soup, 42
    Bacon & Egg Maple Muffins, 39
    Bacon & Sweet Potato Hash, 144
    Best Nut-Free Muffins Around, 156
    Blonde Macaroons, 169
    Blueberry Muffins, 65
    Buffalo Chicken Wings, 55
    Butternut Squash Fritters, 78
    Cauliflower Hummus, 75
    Cauliflower Pizza Bites, 47
    Chicken Maple Sausage Meatballs, 48
    Chocolate Chia Workout Bars, 137
    Chocolate Sunflower Seed Butter, 157
    Chocolate Zucchini "Bread," 164
    Cinnamon Blueberry Bread, 64
    Cinnamon Donut Holes, 174
    Creamy Zucchini, 77
    Crispy Four-Seed Granola, 159
    Crispy Okra Sticks, 68
    Crunchy Omega-3 Flax Granola, 153
    Crunchy Sweet Potato Fries, 138
    Egg Muffins, 51
    Flatbread "PB&J," 158
    Green Deviled Eggs & Bacon, 71
    Homemade Beef Jerky, 43
    introduction to, 33, 148–149
    Kale Salad, 72
    Mexican Muffins, 52
    Minty Thins, 179
    "Peanut Butter" Cookies, 163
    "Peanut Butter" Patties, 155
    Pizza Pockets, 165
    Prosciutto-Wrapped Asparagus, 81
    Pumpkin Chocolate Chip Muffins, 61
    Pumpkin-Spiced Granola Bars, 150
    Silver Dollar Banana Pancakes, 111
    Squash Chips, 82
    Strawberry Gummies, 120
    Sun-Dried Tomato Chicken Sliders, 44
    Superfruity Roll-Ups, 116
    Sweet Bacon Kale, 87
    Sweet & Salty Spiced Pepitas, 160
    Vanilla Cupcakes with Chocolate Frosting, 173
nutritional yeast
    Almond Cheese Crackers, 106
    Easy "Cheese" Kale Chips, 76
    introduction to, 13, 31

O

okra. See Crispy Okra Sticks, 68
olives

Cauliflower Pizza Bites, 47
    Mediterranean Bread, 49
Onion Rings, 83
on-the-go snacks
    Almond Cheese Crackers, 106
    Apple Crisp Chips, 109
    Buttered Saltine Crackers, 108
    Chocolate Almond Squares, 102
    Chocolate Chip Granola Squares, 103
    Chocolate Chip Muffins, 123
    Cinnamon Bun Biscuits, 122
    Cinnamon Graham Crackers, 100
    Cinnamon Raisin Bars, 124
    Crispy Maple Granola, 112
    Flatcake Sandwich Bread, 115
    introduction to, 98–99
    Mini Zucchini Muffins, 125
    My Favorite Crunchy Crackers, 114
    Pinwheel Sandwich Bread, 117
    Pumpkin Bars, 105
    Raw Coconut Almond Bonbons, 119
    Silver Dollar Banana Pancakes, 111
    Strawberry Gummies, 120
    Superfruity Roll-Ups, 116

P

Paleo diet, 12–13
palm shortening, introduction to, 28
Pancake-Wrapped Sausage, 93
Parmesan cheese
    Cauliflower Pizza Bites, 47
    Kale Salad, 72
    Squash Chips, 82
peanut butter
    Mini Peanut Butter Banana Cups, 170
    Paleo diet and, 13
    "Peanut Butter" Cookies, 163
    "Peanut Butter" Patties, 155
    Raw Coconut Almond Bonbons, 119
pecans
    Crispy Maple Granola, 112
    N'Oatmeal Cookies, 180
    Sweet Potato Casserole Bread, 143
pepitas
    Apple Pie Trail Mix Balls, 152
    Best Nut-Free Muffins Around, 156
    Crispy Four-Seed Granola, 159
    Crunchy Granola Brittle, 132
    Crunchy Omega-3 Flax Granola, 153
    introduction to, 23
    Kale Salad, 72
    Mint Chocolate Chip Balls, 168
    Pumpkin-Spiced Granola Bars, 150
    Sweet & Salty Spiced Pepitas, 160
pepperoni
    Cauliflower Pizza Bites, 47
    Pizza Pockets, 165
Perlmutter, David, 39
Pigs in a Blanket, 40
Pinwheel Sandwich Bread, 117
Pizza Pockets, 165
Powerhouse Paleo Coffee, 135
processed foods, 10, 14, 16
Prosciutto-Wrapped Asparagus, 81
protein, 34
psyllium husk powder
    Cinnamon Blueberry Bread, 64
    Cinnamon Bun Biscuits, 122
    Cinnamon Donut Holes, 174
    Flatbread "PB&J," 158
    introduction to, 13, 31
    Pigs in a Blanket, 40

Pizza Pockets, 165
Soft Paleo Pretzels, 88–89
Vanilla Cupcakes with Chocolate Frosting, 173
pumpkin purée
Pumpkin Bars, 105
Pumpkin Chocolate Chip Muffins, 61
Pumpkin-Spiced Granola Bars, 150
pumpkin seeds. *See* pepitas.

R
raisins
Cinnamon Raisin Bars, 124
Mini Zucchini Muffins, 125
N'Oatmeal Cookies, 180
Ranch "Cheese" Ball, 90
raspberries. *See* Superfruity Roll-Ups, 116
Raw Coconut Almond Bonbons, 119
Roasted Red Pepper Dip, 91

S
salmon. *See* Teriyaki Salmon Cakes, 53
salsa. *See* Mexican Muffins, 52
sausage
Egg Muffins, 51
Italian Meatballs, 56
Pancake-Wrapped Sausage, 93
Savory Baked Chicken Nuggets, 36
school and work snacks
Apple Crumb Bites, 59
Bacon Cauliflower Soup, 42
Bacon & Egg Maple Muffins, 39
Blonde Snack Bars, 60
Blueberry Muffins, 65
Buffalo Chicken Wings, 55
Cauliflower Pizza Bites, 47
Chicken Maple Sausage Meatball, 48
Cinnamon Blueberry Bread, 64
Egg Muffins, 51
Homemade Beef Jerky, 43
Italian Meatballs, 56
Mediterranean Bread, 49
Mexican Muffins, 52
Pigs in a Blanket, 40
Pumpkin Chocolate Chip Muffins, 61
Savory Baked Chicken Nuggets, 36
Sun-Dried Tomato Chicken Sliders, 44
Supersmart Bars, 63
Teriyaki Salmon Cakes, 53
sea salt, introduction to, 29
sesame seeds
Ranch "Cheese" Ball, 90
Savory Baked Chicken Nuggets, 36
shredded coconut
Apple Crumb Bites, 59
Apple Pie Trail Mix Balls, 152
Blonde Macaroons, 169
Chocolate Almond Squares, 102
Chocolate Chia Workout Bars, 137
Chocolate Chip Granola Squares, 103
Crispy Four-Seed Granola, 159
Crispy Maple Granola, 112
Crunchy Omega-3 Flax Granola, 153
introduction to, 31
Onion Rings, 83
Pancake-Wrapped Sausage, 93
Pumpkin-Spiced Granola Bars, 150
Raw Coconut Almond Bonbons, 119
Supersmart Bars, 63
silicone cupcake liners, 32
Silver Dollar Banana Pancakes, 111
Snickerdoodle Cookie Dough Bites, 185

Soft Paleo Pretzels, 88–89
spinach
Egg Muffins, 51
Green Lemonade Smoothie, 95
Superfruity Roll-Ups, 116
Squash Chips, 82
stevia, introduction to, 26
strawberries
Flatbread "PB&J," 158
Strawberry Gummies, 120
Superfruity Roll-Ups, 116
Sun-Dried Tomato Chicken Sliders, 44
sunflower seed butter
Apple Pie Trail Mix Balls, 152
Chocolate Zucchini "Bread," 164
Flatbread "PB&J," 158
introduction to, 21
Mini Peanut Butter Banana Cups, 170
"Peanut Butter" Cookies, 163
"Peanut Butter" Patties, 155
sunflower seeds
Best Nut-Free Muffins Around, 156
Blonde Macaroons, 169
Chocolate Chia Workout Bars, 137
Chocolate Sunflower Seed Butter, 157
Crispy Four-Seed Granola, 159
Crunchy Omega-3 Flax Granola, 153
Superfruity Roll-Ups, 116
Supersmart Bars, 63
Sweet Bacon Kale, 87
sweet potatoes
Bacon & Sweet Potato Hash, 144
Crunchy Sweet Potato Fries, 138
Sweet Potato Casserole Bread, 143
Sweet Potato Pancakes, 147
Sweet Potato Power Brownies, 128
Sweet & Salty Spiced Pepitas, 160
sweet treats
Apple Crumble, 183
Blonde Macaroons, 169
"Cheesecake" Bites with Caramel Sauce, 176
Chocolate-Covered Cookies, 184
Cinnamon Donut Holes, 174
Happy Birthday Cookie Cake, 177
introduction to, 166–167
Mini Peanut Butter Banana Cups, 170
Mint Chocolate Chip Balls, 168
Minty Thins, 179
Molten Lava Cakes, 182
N'Oatmeal Cookies, 180
Snickerdoodle Cookie Dough Bites, 185
Vanilla Cupcakes with Chocolate Frosting, 173

T
tahini. *See* Cauliflower Hummus, 75
tamari soy sauce
Homemade Beef Jerky, 43
introduction to, 31
Teriyaki Salmon Cakes, 53
tomatoes
Cauliflower Pizza Bites, 47
Creamy Zucchini, 77
Egg Muffins, 51
Mediterranean Bread, 49
Pizza Pockets, 165
Sun-Dried Tomato Chicken Sliders, 44

V
Vanilla Cupcakes with Chocolate Frosting, 173

W
walnuts
Apple Crumb Bites, 59
Apple Crumble, 183
Artichoke Pesto, 92
Banana Walnut Muffins, 142
Cinnamon Raisin Bars, 124
Crispy Maple Granola, 112
Mini Zucchini Muffins, 125
N'Oatmeal Cookies, 180
Pumpkin Bars, 105
Roasted Red Pepper Dip, 91
Supersmart Bars, 63
Zesty Walnut Brussels Sprouts, 84

Y
yellow squash. See Squash Chips, 82

Z
Zesty Walnut Brussels Sprouts, 84
zucchini
Chocolate Zucchini "Bread," 164
Creamy Zucchini, 77
Mini Zucchini Muffins, 125
Squash Chips, 82

ACKNOWLEDGMENTS

For my sweet husband, Scott. I don't know how to even begin to express my gratitude. You supported me every step of the way as I wrote this book. Your patience, guidance, editing, and most of all love, inspired me day in and day out. Not to mention you have been my best friend and my soul mate for almost thirty years, and I am the most fortunate woman in the world.

For my amazing kiddos, Alice and Tate. This book would not have been possible without you all! You were instrumental in each stage, from cooking, to tasting, to critiquing. Thank you for trying every single recipe with an open mind and giving me your honest opinion, from your "It's not my favorite," response to the uplifting "Wow, Mom, now this is good!" I cherish time spent with you all and I am so blessed to be your mom.

For my neighbor and friend Drennen, who voluntarily served as my full-time taste tester and helper. I can't thank you enough for your help, support, advice, and encouragement throughout this process. I must confess that, for the first time, I am thankful for your "sweet tooth." Through our tasting collaboration (yours sweet, mine salty), I am confident that these recipes will appeal to various tastes and interests.

For my dear friends who cheer me on, encourage me, and believe in me. Thank you! Your friendship and support mean the world to me, and you gave me the confidence to fulfill a dream.

And lastly, thank you to Heather Connell, for opening this door for me, and to Jill Alexander, my editor, for this amazing opportunity.

ABOUT THE AUTHOR

Landria Voigt, C.H.H.C., is a nutritional consultant and public speaker. In her twenties she was diagnosed with an autoimmune disease and for years struggled to keep flares in check with traditional, conventional approaches. After more than a decade of suffering and frustration, she took her health into her own hands, casting aside the drugs and carefully experimenting with her own diet. The results were nothing short of miraculous.

As a result of her journey, she came to appreciate the power of nutrition and how challenging it can be to separate facts from dubious marketing spin when choosing the right foods for one's self and family. Now she is on a mission to help others enjoy healthier living through informed eating. Through public speaking engagements and consulting at The Atlanta Center for Holistic and Integrative Medicine for Dr. Taz's patients in Atlanta, she shares her knowledge and most up-to-date research on the ever-changing subjects of food and wellness.

Through her blog stiritup.me, Landria shares her healthy recipes aimed at pleasing even the most finicky of palates, as well as forward-thinking ideas about nutrition.